MODERN INDIA

OTHER TITLES IN THE COMPARATIVE SOCIETIES SERIES

MODERN INDIA

A Volume in the Comparative Societies Series

JOTI SEKHON
Greensboro College

Boston   Burr Ridge, IL   Dubuque, IA   Madison, WI   New York
San Francisco   St. Louis   Bangkok   Bogotá   Caracas   Lisbon
London   Madrid   Mexico City   Milan   New Delhi   Seoul
Singapore   Sydney   Taipei   Toronto

McGraw-Hill Higher Education

*A Division of The **McGraw-Hill** Companies*

MODERN INDIA

Copyright ©2000 by The McGraw-Hill Companies, Inc. All rights reserved. Printed in the United States of America. Except as permitted under the United States Copyright Act of 1976, no part of this publication may be reproduced or distributed in any form or by any means, or stored in a data base or retrieval system, without the prior written permission of the publisher.

This book is printed on acid-free paper.

1 2 3 4 5 6 7 8 9 0 DOC/DOC 9 0 9 8 7 6 5 4 3 2 1 0 9

ISBN 0-07-292824-7

Editorial director: *Phillip A. Butcher*
Sponsoring editor: *Sally Constable*
Marketing manager: *Leslie A. Kraham*
Editorial assistant: *Kate Purcell*
Project manager: *Kimberly D. Hooker*
Production supervisor: *Michael McCormick*
Designer: *Laurie Entringer*
Compositor: *Shepherd Incorporated*
Typeface: *10/12 Palatino*
Printer: *R. R. Donnelley*

Library of Congress Cataloging-in-Publication Data

Sekhon, Joti.
    Modern India / Joti Sekhon.
       p. cm.—(Comparative societies series)
    Includes bibliographical references.
    ISBN 0-07-292824-7
    1. India. I. Title. II. Series.
DS407.S415 2000
954.04—dc21   99-37247

http://www.mhhe.com

Dedicated to the memory of my father,
Brigadier Harbans Singh Sekhon (1924–1989)
and
my mother, Harsharan Kaur

EDITOR'S PREFACE

In one of the early scenes of the movie *Reds,* the U.S. revolutionary journalist John Reed, just back from covering the beginning of World War I, is asked by a roomful of business leaders, "What is this War really about?" John Reed stands and stops all conversation with a one-word reply—"profits." Today, war between major industrial nations would disrupt profits much more than create money for a military industrial complex. Highly integrated global markets and infrastructures support the daily life of suburban families in Chicago and urban squatter settlements in Bombay. These ties produce a social and economic ecology that transcends political and cultural boundaries.

The world is a very different place than it was for our parents and grandparents. Those rare epic events of world war certainly invaded their everyday lives and futures, but we now find that daily events thousands of miles away, in countries large and small, have a greater impact on North Americans than ever before, with the speed of this impact multiplied many times in recent decades. Our standard of living, jobs, and even prospects of living in a healthy environment have never before been so dependent on outside forces.

Yet there is much evidence that North Americans have less easy access to good information about the outside world than even a few years ago. Since the end of the Cold War, newspaper and television coverage of events in other countries has dropped dramatically. It is difficult to put much blame on the mass media, however: International news seldom sells any more. There is simply less interest.

It is not surprising, then, that Americans know comparatively little about the outside world. A recent *Los Angeles Times* survey provides a good example: People in eight countries were asked five basic questions about current events of the day. Americans were dead last in their knowledge, trailing people from Canada, Mexico, England, France, Spain, Germany, and Italy.* It is also not surprising that the annual report published by the Swiss World Economic Forum always ranks American executives quite low in their international experience and understanding.

Such ignorance harms American competitiveness in the world economy in many ways. But there is much more. Seymour Martin Lipset put it nicely in one of his recent books: "Those who know only

---

*For example, whereas only 3 percent of Germans missed all five questions, 37 percent of the Americans did (*Los Angeles Times,* March 16, 1994).

one country know no country" (Lipset 1996: 17). Considerable time spent in a foreign country is one of the best stimulants for a sociological imagination: Studying or doing research in other countries makes us realize how much we really, in fact, have learned about our own society in the process. Seeing other social arrangements, ways of doing things, and foreign perspectives allows for far greater insight into the familiar, our own society. This is also to say that ignorance limits solutions to many of our own serious social problems. How many Americans, for example, are aware that levels of poverty are much lower in all other advanced nations and that the workable government services in those countries keep poverty low? Likewise, how many Americans are aware of alternative means of providing health care and quality education or reducing crime?

We can take heart in the fact that sociology in the United States has become more comparative in recent decades. A comparative approach, of course, was at the heart of classical European sociology during the 1800s. But as sociology was transported from Europe to the United States early in the 20th century, it lost much of this comparative focus. In recent years, sociology journals have published more comparative research. There are large data sets with samples from many countries around the world in research seeking general laws on issues such as the causes of social mobility or political violence, all very much in the tradition of Durkheim. But we also need much more of the old Max Weber. His was a qualitative historical and comparative perspective (Smelser 1976; Ragin and Zaret 1983). Weber's methodology provides a richer understanding of other societies, a greater recognition of the complexity of social, cultural, and historical forces shaping each society. Ahead of his time in many ways, C. Wright Mills was planning a qualitative comparative sociology of world regions just before his death in 1961 (Horowitz 1983:324). [Too few American sociologists have yet to follow in his footsteps.]

Following these trends, sociology textbooks in the United States have also become more comparative in content in recent years. And while this tendency must be applauded, it is not enough. Typically, there is an example from Japan here, another from Germany there, and so on, haphazardly for a few countries in different subject areas as the writer's knowledge of these bits and pieces allows. What we need are the textbook equivalents of a richer Weberian comparative analysis, a qualitative comparative analysis of the social, cultural, and historical forces that have combined to make relatively unique societies around the world. It is this type of comparative material that can best help people in the United States overcome their lack of understanding about other countries and allow them to see their own society with much greater insight.

The Comparative Societies Series, of which this book is a part, has been designed as a small step in filling this need. We have currently selected 12 countries on which to focus: Japan, Thailand, Switzerland, Mexico, Eritria, Hungary, Germany, China, India, Iran, Brazil, and Russia. We selected these countries as representatives of major world regions and cultures, and each will be examined in separate books written by talented sociologists. All of these basic sociological issues and topics will be covered: Each book will begin with a look at the important historical and geographical forces shaping the society, then turn to basic aspects of social organization and culture. From there each book will proceed to examine the political and economic institutions of the specific country, along with the social stratification, the family, religion, education, and finally urbanization, demography, social problems, and social change.

Although each volume in the Comparative Societies Series is of necessity brief to allow for use as supplementary readings in standard sociology courses, we have tried to assure that this brief coverage provides students with sufficient information to better understand each society, as well as their own. The ideal would be to transport every student to another country for a period of observation and learning. Realizing the unfortunate impracticality of this ideal, we hope to do the next best thing—to at least mentally move these students to a country very different from their own, provide something of the everyday reality of the people in these other countries, and demonstrate how the tools of sociological analysis can help them see these societies as well as their own with much greater understanding.

Harold R. Kerbo
San Luis Obispo, CA
June 1997

AUTHOR'S PREFACE

As a college professor in the United States, I have often struggled to make India comprehensible to American undergraduate students and others. There is little easily accessible scholarship, and for the most part India does not make news in the U.S. media. Writing this book turned out to be a much more challenging task than I had anticipated. The diversity and dynamism of Indian society is matched only by the variety and shifts in scholarship and writing on India. As I worked to make India intelligible, I also found myself learning more about India and my own heritage and identity as an Indian. It turned out to be an exciting, rewarding, and exhausting experience.

Many people contributed to make this book possible. My parents started me on my journey through life by providing a safe, secure, and supportive environment that nurtured my curiosity about people and places. And they continued to support and encourage me when I ventured out on paths well beyond the expectations of most women in India. I dedicate this book to them for their enduring faith in me and in the value of education. My husband, Alan, and son, Imran, have patiently and lovingly sustained me through the seemingly endless hours I spent at home working on this book. Interaction with many people in India, including my sister, brother, friends, activists, and scholars, provided me with numerous ideas that inform this project. I must thank series editor, Harold Kerbo, for his thoughtful comments, encouragement, and patience as I worked on the manuscript. Comments by Susan Chattin and an anonymous reviewer were very helpful in preparing the final draft. The library staff at Greensboro college did a wonderful job of locating and acquiring hard-to-find books and other information.

Joti Sekhon

CONTENTS

MODERN INDIA

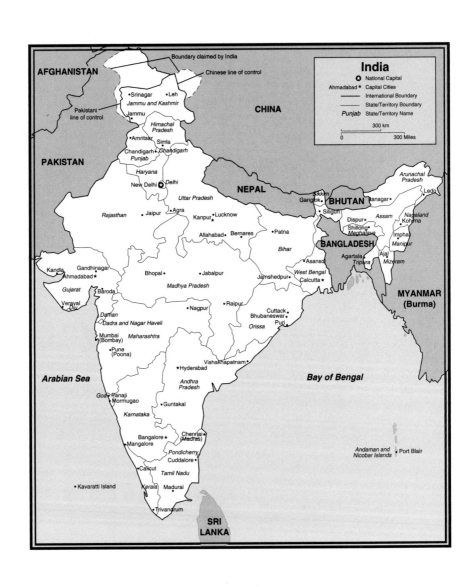

CHAPTER 1

The Indian Puzzle

Visitors from the United States to India may see the golden arches of McDonald's in the Indian capital, New Delhi, and walk in dreaming of Big Mac and fries. Inside they will find items such as "Maharaja Mac," "McAloo Tikki Burger," "Vegetable McNuggets," "McImli Sauce," and "McMasala Sauce." The Maharaja Mac is made with goat meat patties and the word Maharaja means a great king in Hindi. McAloo Tikki is derived from a spiced potato patty, and the sauces are based on Indian chutneys! And, although there are also chicken and fish sandwiches and some other items familiar to North Americans, no beef products are served. The Americans may get frustrated at not getting the juicy Big Mac, but they will also wonder about the capacity of Indians to make a fast-food giant like McDonald's bow to local tastes and use locally produced ingredients. This represented a major change for McDonald's when it opened its first restaurants in India in 1996, as the company markets itself on the distinctiveness and predictability of its products and flavors no matter where franchises are set up.

As with McDonald's, so with much else in India, what at first glance appears familiar and comprehensible turns out to be unfamiliar and incomprehensible soon enough. Nothing is quite the way you expect it to be. The sheer vastness, variety, and unpredictability of this country of one billion inhabitants can be overwhelming. But as the *Lonely Planet* guide to India states, "Love it or hate it you can never ignore India" (Thomas 1997:15).

For centuries India has attracted foreigners by land and sea. In fact Christopher Columbus set out in search of India's legendary wealth and spices when in 1492 he landed instead on a Caribbean island and "discovered" the Americas. That is how the Caribbean islands came to be known as the West Indies and the Native Americans Columbus found here came to be termed Indians! Travelers, scholars, missionaries, and administrators have all attempted to grasp the "essence of India" and failed. This is because the heterogeneity of India cannot be fitted into neatly stacked and labeled boxes. The contents of these boxes somehow always spill over and intermingle to create new and unique cultural patterns and meanings. In many ways India is like a crossword puzzle that cannot be solved, yet one you cannot stop trying to solve!

Historically, for many westerners, India has "evoked a picture of Maharajas, snake-charmers, and the rope-trick" (Thapar 1966:15), even though wealth, mystical activities, and magic were always limited to a very small segment of the population. But when the British consolidated colonial rule over India in the 19th century, the focus turned to everything that was "wrong" with Indian culture and society when compared to Europe. Although there have been more scholarly attempts in recent decades to understand the complex realities in Indian society, few people in North America have much accurate knowledge about India. This is "largely because classical tradition, modern romantic authors, Hollywood films, television and the popular press have combined to portray India in extreme terms: of stunning wealth or abject poverty, of unbridled violence or pacifism, of gross sexuality or spiritualism, and sometimes all the above" (Schwartzberg 1989:1). India offers these extremes, but it also offers much more in-between.

WHAT YOU SEE IN INDIA

You can fly into India on a huge Boeing 747 jumbo jet aircraft, and get on a taxi to take you to your destination. You will at once be confronted with streets crowded by cars, trucks, motorcycles, scooters, mopeds, three-wheeler scooters, buses, bicycles, and pedestrians, all moving at different speeds and jockeying for space. You can travel to different parts of the country, sometimes by airplane or automobile, but more often on trains or buses.

The Indian railway system, started by the British, is legendary, and one of the largest in the world. In fact the state-owned Indian Railway Service is the single largest employer in the world employing over 1.6 million people. Trains range from fast nonstop and air-conditioned ones between some major cities, to express trains that make a few stops. And then you have the numerous "passenger" trains for the masses serving smaller towns and villages. They stop frequently, are unpredictable, and crowded. But it is from the trains that you can see the varied countryside: fields being ploughed by tractors or bullocks; sugar cane, wheat, or rice being sown and harvested using hands or combine harvesters; lush green vegetation, dry shrubbery, and desert sands; goods being transported on carts, tractors, and trucks. Sometimes you can pass by miles of

People at a train station waiting to board a train, a popular means of travel in India.

quiet and peaceful countryside, but you also see people living in various kinds of housing and going about their daily business. Railway stations are always busy. You see travelers coming and going, and people there to receive them or see them off. You see porters carrying baggage on their heads and shoulders, and sometimes on carts. You see vendors selling everything from books and magazines to food and drinks. And you see many people who have made the railway platforms their home!

You can drive on narrow roads up steep hills and mountains to escape the heat, and see the snow-covered Himalayan mountain ranges in the distance. You can see thick forests, but also hillsides stripped of all vegetation. You see water gushing down from the mountains and turning into long, wide, and meandering rivers in the plains. And you can see natural reserves and sanctuaries created to save what's left of India's once-rich forest cover, plant life, and wildlife such as the Bengal tiger, the Asiatic lion, elephants, rhinoceros, and many species of birds.

You can see children dressed in uniforms going to school. You also see them playing hopscotch, cricket, marbles, or local games such as "gulli-danda" using a wooden peg and stick, on the streets. You see them flying kites, or picking through garbage to salvage what they can to sell. You see them working in firecracker, match stick, and carpet factories, and even begging. You see them herding cattle, bathing in streams and irrigation canals. And you see young girls carrying firewood, fetching water, cleaning house, cooking, and minding even younger children.

You see people working with computers, in high-tech industries, on space research, on hydroelectric power plants. You see farmers sitting on beds strung with rope talking on cellular phones. And you see women and men everywhere selling just about everything, vegetables, clothes, household gadgets, consumer goods, electronics, and so forth, on the roadside or in shops of various kinds. You see people participating in political rallies and strikes, or sitting under trees or outside tea stalls engaging in discussions and socializing.

No one can ignore the Indian movies. Massive billboards and posters in bright colors are prominently displayed. The Indian film industry is centered in Bombay, and is popularly referred to as "Bollywood" after Hollywood. India produces more films than any other country, about 800 each year. Films are a major form of mass entertainment often focusing on unrealistic themes. Designed to provide an escape from the rigors of daily life, they are full of romance, song and dance, and melodrama. But you can also see the small but growing number of "new wave" films that attempt to portray some of the realities of Indian life. In addition, Indian classical, folk, and popular music, and dance and theater are to be seen in the numerous festivals and celebrations throughout India.

Indian art, architecture, and handicrafts are legendary. You can see the 2,000-year-old caves at Ajanta and Ellora with Buddhist sculptures and wall paintings in them. You can see the elaborately carved 1,000-year-old Hindu temples at Khajuraho. And you can see the 350-year-old marble and precious-stone masterpiece, the Taj Mahal, that Mughal King Shah Jahan built to memorialize his beloved wife, Mumtaz! You can also see paintings and book illustrations of various kinds. Artisans may be seen weaving a variety of fabrics, embroidering them, decorating them, and fashioning them into decorative covers, pillows, and garments. Metal workers and jewelers craft beautiful patterns on brass, bronze, silver, and gold. Carpet weavers may be seen weaving intricate designs on carpets, while other artisans produce marble and soapstone objects inlayed with precious and semiprecious stones.

WHAT THIS BOOK IS ABOUT

You can see all I have mentioned above and a lot more in India, but you can never know all the complexities that lie beneath the surface. My hope is that this volume starts you on a journey to discover India in its various dimensions, just as writing it is for me just one more phase in my own journey of discovery through India. I use sociological concepts and insights to assist in understanding the vastness and variety that India offers. I start out by introducing the geographic, cultural, and historical background, followed by a deeper understanding of Indian religions. Chapter 4 focuses on caste as the basis of social stratification in India. Indian religions and caste have both generated a lot of interest, but are often misunderstood. The discussion of the relationship between caste and economic status leads into the overview of the Indian economy in

Chapter 5. Gender relations, particularly the position of women, are explored next, followed by the discussion of family patterns, and the role of education in modern India. The dominant role of Indian politics and state institutions in most aspects of social life in modern India is apparent throughout. Chapter 8, therefore, expounds on the political process in India, as well as social movements that are an integral part of Indian politics. India's relations with its neighbors and other countries in the world are also discussed in this chapter. In the concluding chapter, I draw on some themes in earlier chapters and reflect on key aspects of social change in India and challenges for the future.

CHAPTER 2

The Place, the People, and the Past

I think of myself as being "from India" although I have lived in North America since 1982. Indeed, I still retain Indian citizenship. But many of my friends and acquaintances from India are native speakers of languages I do not speak. So we communicate in English, a legacy of British colonial rule in India. And, although my family adheres to the Sikh faith, based mainly in the northern Indian state of Punjab, most Indians I know are Hindus, the dominant religious tradition in India. Largely because my father was inducted by the British into the army, as were numerous Sikhs since the mid-19th century, I have visited, but never lived in, Punjab. As a result, however, I received a relatively privileged and Western-oriented upbringing and education. So I may be "from India" but I illustrate only one element in a geographically, culturally, economically, and politically complex and diverse country shaped by continuous changes over its long recorded history of over 4,000 years. In this chapter I will introduce you to India's geographic location and physical features, provide a glimpse of its cultural diversity, and outline the historical processes through which modern India has emerged.

THE PLACE

India is located at the center of the region known as South Asia or the Indian subcontinent separated from the rest of Asia by various mountain ranges. In addition to India, the region comprises the countries of Pakistan, Bangladesh, Sri Lanka, Nepal, and Bhutan, all of which have emerged from the area that comprised the British Indian Empire until 1947. The physical separation from the rest of the Asian landmass and the physical variations within the region contributed to the development

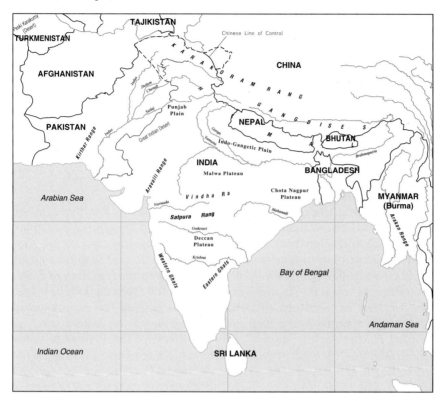

of distinct religious, linguistic, and regional cultures in the subcontinent. Pakistan borders India to the northwest, while China, Nepal, and Bhutan are to the north. Bangladesh is to the east separating most of India from its northeast part, which itself is bordered by Burma. The southern half of India is a peninsula surrounded by the Arabian Sea, the Indian Ocean, and the Bay of Bengal. Separated from the southern tip of India by a narrow strait is the island country of Sri Lanka.

Covering an area of about 1.27 million square miles, India is about one-third the size of the United States. Physically, India is composed of three main regions: the mountainous region comprised mainly of the Himalayas in the north, the Peninsula in the south, and the Indo-Gangetic Plain in-between. The Himalayas, the highest mountain range in the world, include Mount Everest, at 29,028 feet the highest peak in the world, on the border between Nepal and China, and Kanchenjunga at 28,201 feet, on the border between India and Nepal. The Himalayas get lower in height further south, and frame northwestern, north central and northeastern India. The Himalayan region is characterized by plateaus, gorges, and valleys, and is the source of numerous river systems including the Ganga, or Ganges.

The Himalayas give way to the Indo-Gangetic Plain formed by two river systems, the Indus and the Ganga. The Indus River system, extending from Kashmir and Punjab in the north down to the Arabian Sea, is now mostly in Pakistan. Within India, the western part of the Plain is in Punjab and Haryana and stretches east to the state of West Bengal and then turns south into Bangladesh where it is joined by the Brahmaputra River coming from the Assam Valley. The large delta of the Ganga is divided between India and Bangladesh. Characterized by rich alluvial soil, gently sloping land, slow moving rivers, flood plains, and other features related to river systems, the Indo-Gangetic Plain is economically, socially, and politically a very important part of India, and also very densely populated.

Separating the Gangetic Plain from the Deccan Peninsula to the south are the Great Indian Desert or Thar Desert in the state of Rajasthan, and the Central Highlands. These highlands are composed of the Aravalli Range in eastern Rajasthan, and the Vindhya and Satpura Ranges further south. The Narmada River flows between the Vindhya and Satpura Ranges, while the Tapti River is south of the Satpura. Both flow into the Arabian Sea. Historically, these ranges slowed the expansion of northern kingdoms to the south and also allowed the development of distinct cultures in the south. To the northeast of the Peninsula is the Chota Nagpur Plateau in southern Bihar. Most of the interior of the Peninsula is composed of the Deccan Plateau. The Deccan Plateau and the Central Highlands range in height from 300 to 1,800 meters (984–5,904 feet). Flanking the Plateau to the west and east are the Western Ghats and Eastern Ghats, or hills. The Western Ghats are somewhat higher than the Eastern Ghats, and are the source of four major rivers, the Mahanadi, Godavari, Krishna, and Kaveri, that flow east into the Bay of Bengal forming deltas. On either side of the Ghats are fertile and densely populated coastal plains.

Indian rivers, originating mainly in the Himalayas and the Deccan, are of enormous economic and cultural significance. The source of water essential for agricultural development and human life, these rivers have been harnessed for irrigation, flood control, and power generation at various points. The rivers are also prone to periodic flooding resulting in misery and hardship. Their life-giving as well as destructive powers are the basis of numerous legends incorporated into Hindu religious life. Most rivers are considered holy with the Ganga being the holiest. However, the various activities associated with the rivers have implications for the environment, quality of life, and spiritual life, leading to debates and movements on how to manage the waters from the rivers.

Compared to the United States, India is very hot. However, there is a great deal of climatic variation from the north to the south in India, and the weather often changes quickly and dramatically. There is a relatively cool and dry winter from December to February with the north being the coolest, particularly in the Himalayas. Below freezing in the extreme north, the temperature averages about 70 to 80° F in the southern part. The hot and dry summer lasts from March to May and the heat can be oppressive in the later part particularly in the northern and central sections with temperatures ranging from 100 to 120° F. The southwest monsoon bearing warm and moist air from the Arabian Sea and the Bay of Bengal spreads over most of India from June to September. Most of the rain falls during this time with the largest rainfall in the western peninsula and the northeast. A welcome relief from the heat, it is warm and humid nonetheless with daytime highs in the 80 to 95° F range, somewhat similar to the southeastern United States, particularly Florida. The rains provide most of the water for agriculture. However, the amount of rain is unpredictable from year to year leading to both droughts and floods, and causing great anxiety. As the southwest monsoon withdraws and most of India starts getting cooler and drier, the northeast monsoon brings some rains to the Deccan Peninsula during October and November.

THE PEOPLE

In 1999, India's population was about 983 million making it the second most populated country in the world following China with a population of 1.2 billion. The United States was a distant third at about 268 million. India's population, accounting for about 17 percent of the total world population of 5.8 billion, is expected to reach one billion by the year 2000, and overtake that of China in the next decade. And, although India is approximately one-third the size of the United States, its population is almost four times that of the United States, making for a population density of about 750 per square mile in India compared to about 72 per square mile in the United States. India is, therefore, much more crowded than the United States, although population density is highest in the plains and irrigated areas, and in the cities. However, nearly 75 percent of the population lives in rural areas.

The earliest inhabitants of India are believed to be various aboriginal tribes who now live mainly in the hills and plateaus and constitute approximately 3 percent of the population. About 25 percent of Indians are believed to be Dravidians who developed the Indus Valley civilization, or Harappan culture as it is now termed, that flourished between 3000 and 1500 B.C. They were eventually pushed to the south of India by the Indo-European linguistic groups believed to be from Central Asia who established themselves over northern India. They are commonly referred to as Indo-Aryans, and now constitute about 72 percent of Indians.

The numerous languages spoken in India fall into four main linguistic groups: Indo-European, Dravidian, Sino-Tibetan, and Austric.

The exact number of languages and dialects varies according to the sources and method of counting, ranging between 179 and 188 languages, and 49 and 544 dialects. For official use the Constitution of India recognizes 18 languages: Assamese, Bengali, Gujarati, Hindi, Kannada, Kashmiri, Konkani, Malayalam, Manipuri, Marathi, Nepali, Oriya, Punjabi, Sanskrit, Sindhi, Tamil, Telugu, and Urdu. About 112 "mother tongues" are officially recognized as spoken by more than 10,000 people each, and 33 languages are spoken by more than a million people each. The four main Dravidian languages are Kannada, Telegu, Tamil, and Malayalam. The Austric languages probably originating in Indochina, and the Sino-Tibetan languages originating in China, have mostly been absorbed into the Indo-European and Dravidian language groups. But some speakers of Austric languages are to be found among the tribal dwellers of the Chota Nagpur Plateau and Assam Hills in eastern India. Sino-Tibetan speakers are to be found in remote Himalayan regions and in the eastern hills. Most people in the northern two-thirds of India speak the various Indo-European languages derived from Sanskrit, accounting for about 75 to 80 percent of Indians. Hindi is the largest language group comprising about 30 to 40 percent of the Indian population.

About 82 percent of Indians adhere to the Hindu religion, whereas 12 percent are Muslims. Sikhs and Christians constitute about 2 percent of the population each, and Buddhists, Jains, and others, such as Zoroastrians, Jews, and followers of some tribal religions, account for less than 1 percent of the population each. However, the religious landscape in India is complicated by numerous differences among adherents to each faith, such as those of **class, caste, gender,** language, and region. All of these interact to shape modern India.

THE PAST

No attempt to grasp the essential features of Indian culture and society can fail to underscore the diversity and richness of India's past and present. Over a period of more than 4,000 years of recorded history, certain enduring traditions have emerged even as they have changed historically through a complex interplay of the movement of various groups of people into the region and the numerous local traditions. Furthermore, at every point in time and in every part of the region there has been more material as well as ideological diversity than most histories of India cared to acknowledge until recently (Bose and Jalal 1998).

Early India: Pre-2500 B.C. to A.D. 700

The earliest inhabitants are believed to have migrated into India between 200,000 and 400,000 years ago. In the North they probably arrived over the mountains from Central or East Asia, whereas in peninsular India they are believed to have arrived by sea from East Africa. Evidence points to the existence of a village culture in the region in and around the Indus River Valley, most of which is now in Pakistan and from which India derives its current name. Although we have considerable knowledge about the Indus Valley civilization, there is also archaeological evidence of human habitation in other parts of India at the same time (Thapar 1966:25–27).

The Indus Valley later became the site of an urban civilization centering around the cities of Harappa and Mohenjo-daro from about 2500 to 1500 B.C. The Indus Valley civilization, or Harappa culture, was developed by the Dravidians whose origins are not known with certainty, but they are believed to be similar to the Mediterranean people. The economy was based on agriculture with wheat as the main crop. Rice, peas, dates, and mustard were also grown, and a variety of domestic animals were also raised. Archaeological excavations in Harappa, Mohenjo-daro, and more recently in Ganweriwala reveal a literate and highly skilled culture. Seals found at the sites bear pictorial symbols and inscriptions that are yet to be deciphered. The cities were well planned and laid out, and strong brick structures have been found. Activities included fashioning of articles made of pottery, bronze, and copper, as well as spinning and weaving of cotton yarn and cloth. The earliest evidence of using cotton for clothing is to be found here (Wolpert 1993:19). Trade flourished with other parts of the region as well as the Persian Gulf region and Mesopotamia. A priest-king is believed to have ruled the civilization with the assistance of a bureaucracy. It is during this period that some of the earliest evidence of the worship of the deity **Shiva** as a symbol of fertility, creativity, as well as destruction is to be found. These symbols were incorporated into what later came to be known as Hinduism (Wolpert 1993:14–23).

Sometime after 1750 B.C. Harappa culture started to decline probably as a result of a series of natural disasters such as floods, earthquakes, and changes in the course of the Indus River, as well as the migration of new groups of people with less sophisticated technological, administrative, and economic skills. Around 1500 B.C. people speaking Indo-European languages known as Aryans started arriving through the Hindu Kush mountains in the northwest from the region between the Caspian and Black Seas in Central Asia. These seminomadic pastoralists eventually settled into small villages primarily as agriculturalists. Other occupations, such as metallurgy, pottery, weaving, and commercial trading, also grew. With a king as ruler, the Aryans early on were mainly divided into three social categories: the warriors and aristocrats, the priests, and the common people composed of agriculturalists, traders, cattle raisers, and so forth. These categories formed the basis of what later became a complex system of hereditary occupational specialization known as the

caste system. Later, a fourth social category composed of those performing tasks considered menial was added. However, during the early centuries of Aryan presence in India, membership in the occupational groups was not hereditary or inflexible (Thapar 1966:37–38).

Some of the hymns of the **Rig Veda,** the ancient literary and philosophical texts believed to be the basis of Brahmanism that went on to become Hinduism as interpreted by the dominant elites, were written during the first 500 years of this period. The philosophical and abstract Brahmanic interpretation of spiritual and social life, however, coexisted with the widespread appeal of non-Aryan symbols of fertility as well as nature worship and animism among the ordinary people. In subsequent centuries new forms of worship were added, and the religion that later came to be known as Hinduism developed as a result of continuous interplay of plurality of forms of worship and the dominant philosophical strains. The Aryans also introduced the Indo-Aryan language, Sanskrit, in which the *Rig Veda* and later Brahmanic texts were written. Sanskrit, the language of the upper classes, also formed the basis of vernacular languages that later developed in different parts of the northern half of India (Thapar 1966:40–49).

Between 1000 and 450 B.C. the Aryans gradually spread to the east and south. During this time much of northern India was divided into several "tribal oligarchies" or "republics," and by the sixth century B.C. 16 kingdoms also existed (Wolpert 1993:48). The republics were mainly in the Himalayan foothills and the Northwest; the kingdoms or monarchies were established in the Gangetic Plain. It was during this time period, especially in the monarchies, that a more orthodox form of Brahmanism became dominant, and the fourfold classification of people became more inflexible and hereditary in membership. The **Brahmans,** or priests were at the top of the hierarchy, followed in order by the **Kshatriyas** or warriors, the **Vaishyas** or merchants and agriculturalists, and the **Shudras** or servants. Within each of these four **varnas,** as the four categories were termed, there were several **jatis** or sub-castes representing specific occupational groups within a certain rank (Bose and Jalal 1998:15). There were also some groups placed outside the varna scheme who were considered **untouchable** because they perform tasks considered impure and polluting. The republics had a more democratic political and social system where individuality and unorthodox ideas were tolerated. Opposition and challenges to Brahmanism first emerged in the republics. It was here during the sixth century B.C. that two of the most significant philosophical challenges to Brahmanic Hinduism emerged in the form of Buddhism and Jainism (Thapar 1966:50–69).

The center of political power moved further east to Magadha in the area now known as Bihar, where the Mauryan Empire was founded in 321 B.C. and ruled for 140 years. Under the rule of its first three monarchs, Chandragupta, Bindusara, and Ashoka, over a period of 90 years, the

Mauryan Empire united most of India except the three southernmost Dravidian kingdoms of Kerala, Chola, and Pandya. The Mauryans established
an efficient centralized system of government to manage its mainly agricultural society. They also developed trade and commerce as well as the
arts. Ashoka converted to Buddhism apparently because of remorse and
revulsion at the human misery and destruction caused by his wars and
conquests. Under his patronage Buddhism spread, along with its philosophy of non-violence, or **ahimsa,** as well as vegetarianism. The Northwest,
meanwhile, remained more open to West Asian, Persian, and Greek influences. There was increasing trade leading to the growth of towns and craft
guilds, as well as new ideas. Alexander of Macedonia also launched a two-
year campaign in India reaching as far as Punjab (Thapar 1966:70–91).

After the demise of the Mauryan Empire in 185 B.C. most of India
became fragmented politically for the next 500 years. Bactrians and
Greeks were dominant in the northwestern republics, and numerous
kingdoms rose and fell in the northern, central, and southern regions.
However, this period also witnessed unprecedented economic and cultural developments all over India. Trade links with the Roman Empire,
the Greeks, and China flourished especially in the Northwest. And it was
in the first century A.D. that Christianity was first introduced into India.
Greek and Roman architectural influences appeared and Indian ideas influenced the Greco-Roman society.

The Brahmanic form of Hinduism became more organized and
stronger between 200 B.C. and A.D. 300. Philosophically and theoretically,
various cults and rituals were incorporated into the idea of a universal
soul, reflecting a trend toward monotheism, although three main gods,
Brahma, Vishnu, and Shiva, symbolized different aspects of spiritual
and human existence. At the same time, however, popular cults and local
forms of spiritual expression, including fertility cults and worship of the
mother goddess, also flourished. A new form of worship called **bhakti** or
devotion was introduced for the first time, and later became very popular with the non-Brahmans as well as women. In theory, the rules governing social interaction between the castes became more rigid and acquired Brahmanic ritual sanction. The status of women also declined. But
many variations and modifications existed in practice (Wolpert
1993:80–84; Thapar 1966:131–34).

Formal education focused on learning Sanskrit and studying the
Vedic texts written in Sanskrit, but was limited primarily to Brahmans
and the elite. Vocational training and technical education, though, were
open to artisans and professionals through the guilds. Other popular
Indo-Aryan languages also grew. Art and architecture received financial
backing mainly from the merchants and guilds, but also through royal
patronage. Buddhist art, architecture, and religion were encouraged the
most. As Buddhism became more influential and spread, it also became
exposed to new ideas and changed.

Increasingly, the mountain ranges and hilly terrain separating southern India from the North became less of a barrier and there was more cultural and economic interaction between the North and the South. Aryan influences reached the South in the form of Brahmanism, ideas of hereditary kingship, administrative and revenue systems, and commercial development. Trade and commerce flourished both by sea from the two southern coasts and by land in the North, leading to the development of strong merchant classes and the increased ideological and political influence of the guilds (Thapar 1966:122–31).

It was not until A.D. 320 that northern India was once again united under the Gupta Empire and remained united till the mid-seventh century, except during the last half of the sixth century. This period is often referred to as "the classical age" of Hinduism, and indeed of India. Brahmanic Hinduism and Vedic rituals received royal patronage, and Hindu temple architecture reached the height of its splendor. However, the Gupta kings exercised a decentralized form of control, and were tolerant and flexible toward other religions and social practices, so Buddhism and Jainism also flourished. Both Hinduism and Buddhism spread along with trade and commerce with East and Southeast Asia. Over time, however, Hinduism declined in other parts of Asia and Buddhism became very popular.

In the south of India, meanwhile, the various kingdoms, such as the Pandyas, Cholas, and Pallavas promoted the spread of Brahmanic Hinduism, and many Dravidian influences traveled north. Local forms of religious expression such as bhakti, goddess worship, and fertility cults, however, continued to develop and flourish, and later spread to the North. The "classical age" also witnessed the development of literature in both Sanskrit and Prakrit, the vernacular language popular among the larger population. Agriculture remained an important economic activity, but textile manufacturing in silk, cotton, wool, muslin, linen, and calico became significant.

India's early history, therefore, reflects a dynamic and changing society, along with an ability to accommodate tremendous cultural, economic, and philosophical diversity. In the subsequent centuries, the region went on to meet the challenge of accommodating Islam, which eventually became an integral part of the Indian cultural and historical process.

Regional States and the Rise of Islamic Influence

The period between the 8th and the 16th centuries is characterized by the activities of several regional states and the development of local cultures in most parts of India, as well as the gradual spread of Islamic power and influence over much of northern India starting with the Northwest.

Arabs turned their attention toward India soon after the emergence of Islam in Saudi Arabia in A.D. 622, and the first significant conquest was in Sind, now in Pakistan, in A.D. 711. Muslim rule, however, was limited to Sind till the late 10th century. In other parts of northern India, various states, such as the Palas, Pratiharas, Rashtrakutas, and several Rajput states, fought among themselves, with the Rajputs in the central part increasing their power during the 9th and 10th centuries.

These regional states looked inward, and developed and celebrated their local cultures. The village emerged as the largely self-sufficient unit of production. A feudal system, under which a part of the produce was paid to the landholders and the kings, discouraged production of a surplus, leading to a decline in trade with the outside world. Artisans continued to work in towns and villages, but the guilds declined in power and importance. There was an overall decline in economic well-being and a rise of money lenders and debt. Occupational specialization contributed to the emergence of numerous sub-castes that were incorporated into the fourfold caste hierarchy as legitimized by the Brahmans. Jainism and Buddhism declined in popularity. Brahmanic Hinduism was practiced by the elite, whereas popular Hinduism incorporated elements of Brahmanism and more personalized images of the gods and deities in their religious practices. Sanskrit remained the language of the courts and the elite even as other vernacular Indo-Aryan languages such as Gujarati, Marathi, Bengali, and Assamese developed (Thapar 1966:241–265).

This pattern of political and social organization was shattered by the invasions of the Turkish ruler, Mahmud, of Ghazni in Afghanistan starting at the end of the 10th century in the Northwest, and Rajendra Chola's campaign north along the east coast on to the eastern Gangetic Plain. Mahmud raided western India several times until A.D. 1030, looting and destroying Hindu temples and torturing and killing Hindus. He annexed Punjab and developed Ghazni as a wealthy center of Islamic culture. Turkish and Afghan raids continued expanding further east and south until in A.D. 1206 Qutb-ud-din Aybak declared himself the sultan or ruler of Delhi, the present-day capital of India. Five Muslim dynasties ruled various parts of northern and central India over a period of 320 years as part of the Delhi Sultanate culminating in the formation of the powerful Mughal Empire in 1526. Hindu kingdoms in the South put up varying degrees of resistance, one example being the kingdom of Vijayanagar founded in 1336. During the 14th and 15th centuries some Muslim chiefs in the periphery of the Delhi Sultanate also declared independence (Thapar 1966:266–88).

During this time, an Indo-Muslim culture developed based on accommodation and interaction between Hindu and Muslim ways of life mostly in the North, but also in the South. Some common patterns emerged that were conducive to the eventual political unification of India under the Mughals, and later the British. Initially the Muslims were small in numbers and had to rely on local Hindu converts to Islam to assist in administering their domain. These converts, mainly lower-caste Hindus such as artisans and cultivators attracted by an egalitarian Islamic philosophy, retained many local customs including some features of the caste system. Upper-caste Hindus and upper-class Muslims, however, stayed quite isolated from one another. They also were more concerned about "protecting" their women, which led to increased isolation and **purdah** or veiling. Artisan and peasant women had more freedom mainly because of their important role in economic production. Among the Muslims, the foreign-born or descendants of Arab, Turk, Afghan, and Persian Muslims were ranked the highest, followed by the upper-caste Hindu converts, and then the lower occupational castes.

Religious rituals in mosques and temples became more orthodox as both Muslim and Hindu elites attempted to maintain a distinction between the two faiths and preserve their respective customs and traditions. However, among Hindus the Bhakti movement spread further north by the 14th century and was influenced by a form of Islamic mysticism called **Sufism** that came to India during the 13th century. Both appealed to the poorer and lower-caste masses, focusing on intense personal devotion to god, and both critiqued human suffering and hierarchical social relations. Two of the most significant Bhakti saints of the 15th century were Kabir and Nanak. Nanak, born in 1469 in Punjab, combined strains of Bhakti and Sufi philosophies to found what developed into the Sikh religion (Bose and Jalal 1998:23–34; Thapar 1966:289–320).

Although there was also some cross-fertilization in the spheres of administration, art, and architecture, the key changes were in the cultural arena. Thapar (1966:319) notes, "it is evident that a synthesis of the two cultures took place, although this synthesis did not occur at every level and with the same intensity." Between 1200 and 1526 Islamic influence spread to the south, coming not only from the north but also by sea through trade with the Arab regions. Toward the end of this period many Deccan kings also started trade with Europeans.

The Mughal Empire and Arrival of Europeans

Babur, the Turkish ruler of Kabul in Afghanistan, established the Mughal Empire in northern India in 1526 and passed it on to his son, Humayun, in 1530. However, it was Humayun's son, Akbar, who ascended the throne in 1556, and over the course of the next half-century consolidated the empire. The Mughal Empire was at the height of its power during the 17th century when it expanded to cover most of what is now India, Pakistan, and Bangladesh. Initially characterized by Western scholars as a classic example of "oriental despotism," recent historical research suggests that the Mughal period may be more appropriately "viewed as a complex, nuanced and loose form of hegemony over a diverse, differentiated and dynamic economy and society" (Bose and Jalal 1998:36).

Akbar's reign is characterized by his recognition of India's diversity and tolerance of all faiths. As Muslims were numerically a minority, Akbar needed the cooperation of Hindus for effective administration. He granted them administrative positions, such as those of ministers, military chiefs, and provincial governors, in exchange for service and loyalty. He also abolished many of the taxes imposed by earlier Muslim rulers on Hindus. Although a Muslim, his court ceremonies reflected Sufi mysticism rather than orthodox Islam. He also organized philosophical and theological debates among representatives of different faiths. Akbar established a complex and well-organized administrative system, called the **Mansabdari** system under which individuals were paid cash to raise and maintain a cavalry for use by the emperor for civil and military purposes. About 70 percent of the officeholders were foreign-born Muslims, but 30 percent were local Muslims and Hindus. He also divided the empire into provinces, districts, and subdistricts for efficient management and revenue collection. These administrative divisions, with some modifications, formed the basis of administration under British rule and in post-independence India. Trade and commerce expanded although agricultural production was largely for subsistence with most of the surplus going to pay taxes and duties. Revenue collectors amassed considerable wealth that they mostly used for consumption. But the peasants were generally well off compared to their European counterparts under feudalism. Akbar encouraged the spread of Persian cultural and literary influence, but he also patronized Hindu art, architecture, and literature, especially Rajput styles from central India (Spear 1978:26–51).

Much of this pattern continued during the 17th century under Akbar's successors. The fusion of Persian and Hindu art and architecture is evident in many surviving structures of the period, including the Red Fort and Jama Masjid (mosque) in Delhi, and the famous Taj Mahal in Agra, near Delhi, that was built by Akbar's grandson, Shah Jahan, during his reign from 1628 to 1648. Persian remained the official court language, but Urdu, a language based mostly on the Hindi dialects combined with Arabic and Persian words, and Persian script, became a more popular language of Indo-Islamic culture in northern India. Significant developments in Indian classical music also took place during this time.

The Mughals remained fairly tolerant for most of the 17th century except during the latter part of Aurangzeb's reign from 1658 to 1707. Aurangzeb reverted to a more orthodox Islam and reimposed many taxes on wealthier Hindus and people from other faiths, mainly to generate resources needed to defend the empire. It was during this century that Sikhism changed from a peaceful devotional faith to a more militant group organized in defense of their faith, and Sikhs have since remained important players in northern Indian society and politics. Increasingly during the 17th century, the Mughal political dominance was also challenged in the Northwest by other Muslim rulers, and in central and southern India by the Hindus. After Aurangzeb's death in 1707 there was decline in the size and power of the Mughals, and the last Mughal king was finally deposed by the British in 1857. However, bankers and merchants became powerful, and the economy remained dynamic, although economic prosperity was unevenly distributed. Tremendous cultural and spiritual diversity continued to exist (Bose and Jalal 1998:48–56).

Even as the Mughals were consolidating their power, European voyages to India started setting the stage for eventual British colonial rule. The Portuguese navigator, Vasco da Gama, sailed into the southwestern Indian coast port of Calicut on May 27, 1498, in order to control the lucrative spice trade and to spread Christianity. The Portuguese established Portuguese Catholicism, but their influence was limited to the region around Goa. The Dutch became dominant traders in southern India during the 17th century over which time period the British East India Company also tried to gain a foothold in India. The British became more successful in the northern part of the western coast in Gujarat around the port of Surat and entered into a trade alliance with the Mughals. Later in the 17th century the British moved further up the east coast of India at the expense of the Dutch, and on to Calcutta, even as they received more support from the British monarchy. Over the course of the 18th century the British competed with the French, and were aided in obtaining dominance by French defeats in Europe. They gained control over the port of Madras, now Chennai, after the treaty of Aix-la-Chapelle in 1749, and Bengal after the Seven Years' War from 1756 to 1763.

Transition to British Colonial Dominance

In the course of the next 100 years, the British gradually established colonial rule over most of India, interestingly during a time when European colonization in the Americas was ending. India became Britian's largest and most lucrative colonial possession. Although the regional states in India put up varying degrees of resistance, the British were often able to form alliances with Indian merchants and bankers who sought more independence from local rulers, as well as access to external trade that was controlled by Europeans. Robert Clive, as head of the East India Company, first exploited local rivalries to obtain free access to trade, tax exemptions, and eventually revenue collection and administrative rights over Bengal and much of eastern India. By the middle of the 19th century, the East India Company, with the support of the British government, established effective direct and indirect control over most of India. They engaged in military operations with the warrior states, such as

Mysore, the Marathas, and Sikhs. In 1848, the Sikhs in Punjab became the last group to be subdued. Rulers of some states were allowed to remain somewhat independent but under overall British control. They set in motion a series of economic, political, administrative, and social changes, thereby altering key aspects of Indian society.

Lord Cornwallis, appointed governor general in 1785, instituted a centralized bureaucracy, with Europeans filling the upper administrative positions assisted by Indians at the middle and lower levels. The main concern was with revenue collection, and the system of land control was altered for that purpose. Until now, many of the people with rights to the land, called **zamindars,** were appointed by the Mughals to collect taxes and maintain law and order. But they were not private owners of landed property. Under the Permanent or *Zamindari* Settlement of 1793, modeled on the European system, the zamindars were granted private ownership rights over these lands in exchange for a certain percentage as tax. As a result of floods, droughts, and high-revenue demands, however, most zamindars were not able to pay their share of the revenue. Urban Hindu bankers and moneylenders often took over the lands and emerged as absentee landlords, who also became loyal British subjects. The peasants were particularly hard hit, and a more settled and less mobile rural Indian society emerged, making it easier for the British to achieve control.

During the first half of the nineteenth century, the British initiated the development of a modern infrastructure, such as roads, railroads, canals for irrigation, and postal and telegraph communications. This allowed the opening of many parts of India to the outside world, a process accelerated in subsequent decades. Indian products, particularly raw materials could be exported, and Indian markets were opened up to cotton textiles and other British manufactured products. This started the process of displacement of the Indian textile industry in particular, and stifled industrial development in India. The weavers and artisans, especially, were hurt badly.

Although the British were not overtly concerned with transforming the local social, economic, and political system at this stage, their selective intervention did lead to fundamental transformations. Many aspects of a flexible and varied sociocultural landscape were solidified. For example, Hindu and Muslim religious texts written by the elite and orthodox segments, were often used for moral guidance, but ignored or modified in practice. The British, however, accorded caste hierarchy and rituals more legitimacy and substance, and codified the Muslim **Sharia** into strict law (Bose and Jalal 1998:76). The British also encouraged the arrival of Christian missionaries as well as new policies aimed at promoting Western ideas and institutions in religion, science, education, and economic organization. English replaced Persian as the language of official business although local languages were promoted at the lower administrative levels. Some upper-caste and upper-class Indian elites who assisted the British acquired a Western outlook that they incorporated into their Hindu culture (Spear 1978:125–28).

As the British expanded their control over India and instituted new policies, there were resistance, opposition, and discontent, particularly from the peasants, zamindars, and tribal populations. The most serious challenge was the revolt started in 1857 by Hindu and Muslim soldiers in the town of Meerut, near Delhi, which spread to several other parts of northern and central India. The unrest, termed a "mutiny" by the British and India's first "war of independence" by Indian nationalists, continued until late 1858 when the rebellion was finally crushed. The British crown officially ended the rights of the East India Company, and took direct control of India as part of the British Empire with Queen Victoria as the Empress. A variety of factors contributed to the rebellion. Many Indian aristocrats were anxious to end British rule. There was also resentment over the introduction of Western ideas and institutions, and a perception among Hindus and Muslims that there was an effort to impose Christianity. Moreover, there was increasing opposition at the displacement of the peasantry and landholders as a result of British economic policies (Spear 1978:139–43; Bose and Jalal 1998:88–96).

After the revolt of 1857–58, the British consolidated their rule, but were more sensitive to the opinions of the Indian elite, and less overt in their interference in local customs and traditions. The British Indian army was reorganized with the induction of recruits from groups that had proved to be loyal, such as the Sikhs, Rajputs, Pathans, and Gurkhas. Their military skills were attributed to their being labeled "martial races," as opposed to those who resisted the British (and were subdued) and who were termed "effeminate." The British, however, accelerated the process of infrastructural development, such as irrigation, railroads, communication networks, mainly aimed at the production of Indian raw materials like jute, cotton, coffee, tea, and wheat for export. British manufactured goods and finished products, such as machinery and textiles, were imported. Much of the wealth generated as a result was transfered to Britain or used to maintain the empire.

The Rise of Indian Nationalism

As the British consolidated their direct rule over India in the 19th century, movements for Indian cultural revival and reform, and nationalism emerged. Exaltation of some elements of India's rich cultural heritage was combined with a critique and reform of certain aspects, such as caste hierarchies, Brahmanic rituals, child marriage, **polygamy,** and low status of women and widows. However, the reformers upheld the key philosophical ideas underlying Hinduism that allowed all to lead a humane life and tolerated diverse forms of spiritual expression. Some sections of the mostly high caste and urban Indian elite created by the British, and influenced by Western education and ideas, led this reform movement. For instance, Ram Mohun Roy founded the *Brahmo Samaj* or Society of Brahma in 1828 in Calcutta, and Dayanand Saraswati founded the *Arya Samaj* in 1875 in Bombay (now Mumbai). Sir Sayyid Ahmad Khan, an upper-class Muslim from Delhi, argued for the liberalization of Islam. The urban reformers did not see a contradiction between the Western ideas of reason, freedom and liberty, and Hindu, Islamic, or Sikh and other Indian philosophies and ways of life. In fact, they argued, the British could apply these same ideas to grant more freedom, liberty, and opportunities to their Indian subjects. There were also urban industrial protests against European economic domination, while in rural areas there were revolts against revenue and tenant laws as well as destruction of tribal lands and livelihood (Bose and Jalal 1998:115).

As various movements emerged, the Indian National Congress (INC) held its first meeting in Bombay in December 1885 and eventually led India to independence from the British in 1947. The leaders launched a political movement calling for more political, civil, and human rights, and improvement in the economic condition of Indians. They demanded more representation in governance and administrative services as well as limits on foreign products in order to encourage Indian-made products. In the early 20th century, however, opposition to British rule ranged from using moderate, peaceful, and constitutional means, to boycott of British-made products; some argued for a violent and revolutionary overthrow of colonial rule. The movement turned more radical between 1905 and 1920, after which focus shifted to driving the British out of India.

British administrators instituted partial reforms while repressing many of the protests, often leading to more demands and protests. For example, in 1905, the partition of the eastern province of Bengal led to the creation of a Hindu majority population in West Bengal, while East Bengal (now Bangladesh) emerged as mostly Muslim in population. Congress opposition to the partition of Bengal was interpreted by many Muslims as an indication that the Congress really represented Hindu interests even though it claimed to be inclusive. This instigated the founding in December 1906 of the All-India Muslim League which eventually led the movement for the partition of British India and the formation of Pakistan in 1947. Ideological divisions and differences over policies, meanwhile, emerged within the INC (Spear 1978:174–77). Under the Indian Councils Act of 1909, the British for the first time allowed the formation of elected legislative councils to allow limited self-government. However, separate electorates were designated for Muslims to ensure their representation in areas where they were the majority, even though Bengal was reunited in 1911.

At the start of the First World War in 1914, the Congress supported the British war effort, and Indian soldiers fought and died in large numbers in Africa, the Middle East, and Europe. However, the war was a major drain on resources and Indian support was not rewarded with more political freedom and economic improvements. The few concessions made by the British were deemed unsatisfactory as Indian Hindu and Muslim aspirations increased. It was also during this period, in 1915, that Mohandas Karamchand Gandhi returned after a two-decade stay in South Africa, and emerged as a leading figure in the movement for independence from British colonial rule.

Gandhi and the Movement for Independence

Gandhi, born in 1869 in the state of Gujarat in western India to a well-off merchant caste family, went to Britain as a young man to study law. He returned to India for a couple of years before moving to Natal in South Africa in 1893 where there was a small Indian community. There he became active in opposing white racism and developed a philosophy of non-violent noncooperation that he used as the basis of his activism against British authorities. He argued that human beings need to search for truth or *satya* by developing and following their inner voices, and through self-discipline and self-realization. In practical terms, this could be achieved through freedom from domination, whether foreign or caste based, simple living, self-reliance and non-violence. Gandhi critiqued several aspects of orthodox Hinduism, particularly the practice of untouchability in the Indian caste system. He renamed those groups defined as untouchable **Harijans** or people of god. He worked for religious harmony and tolerance and until the end fought hard against the partition of India and Pakistan. Giving up wearing Western clothes, Gandhi chose a simple lifestyle and committed himself to India's struggle for independence. Starting with the 1920s, he traveled the country tirelessly, including the villages, gathering a large following and turning the nationalist movement into a mass movement. As a Congress leader, Gandhi negotiated endlessly with the British, the Muslim League, and the various factions of the Congress. He launched several movements of non-violent civil disobedience and noncooperation, such as fasts, strikes, boycotts of foreign goods, tax boycotts, breaking laws deemed unfair, and so on.

Gandhi's movement for independence emerged within the context of large-scale resentment of the British and popular ferment among the peasants, tribals, workers, and youth in rural and urban areas somewhat independent of the Congress. In fact Gandhi and the Congress often had to respond to popular pressures, tried to keep tensions under control, and chose issues for protest that would not lead to religious, caste, and class tensions. Even so, the Congress split along radical and conservative lines, and by the late 1920s more radical movements emerged, and the pace picked up in the early 1930s because of economic crises brought on by the global economic depression. Caste, class, and religious tensions also increased (Bose and Jalal 1998:135–44).

The INC demanded complete independence, and as part of the Government of India Act of 1935, the British accepted the goal of dominion status for India. India was to have a federal structure to allow for regional diversities and provincial autonomy managed by a strong central government. Under the leadership of Jawaharlal Nehru, an English-educated westernized elite, the Congress formed governments in most states following the elections of 1937 except in some parts of Bengal, Sind, and Punjab that had a significant Muslim population. The Congress, plagued by internal factions and divisions, failed to govern effectively. The Muslim League under Muhammad Ali Jinnah believed that majority rule limited rights of minorities, and accused the Congress of favoring Hindu interests.

The Muslim League thereafter consistently campaigned for the creation of a separate country of Pakistan. The start of the Second World War in 1939 resulted in the British dissolving the legislative assemblies and turning their attention to the war effort. Gandhi, meanwhile, continued the movement against Britain for independence and actively argued for a single Indian state. Although many opposed the British war effort, most Indians remained apathetic, and many, such as those in the army, played an important role in the war. India was also a major supply center. Economic activities associated with the war benefited some sectors such as the merchants and industrialists. However, the Indian masses suffered because of high inflation and shortages of essential commodities (Wolpert 1993:329–39).

After the end of the war in 1945 attention turned to debates over how, when, and to whom power should be transferred, and the nature of the political and administrative structure that would emerge. In April 1946, the British proposed a loose federation of states, which would retain some local autonomy and accommodate cultural diversities, while being coordinated by a central government with responsibility over certain key functions. The Congress at first appeared to favor this proposal, but eventually rejected it fearing tensions and the possibility of a weak central government. The Muslim League stepped up its campaign for a separate Muslim state of Pakistan, and riots broke out between the different religious communities in areas with significant mixed populations such as Punjab, Sind, and Bengal. The British were compelled to accept the partition of India, much to the dismay of Gandhi

Power was transferred to the Muslim League led by Jinnah in the new state of Pakistan carved out of the Muslim majority regions of western India and the eastern part of Bengal in the East on August 14, 1947.

India attained independence at the stroke of midnight of August 15, 1947, led by the Indian National Congress with Jawaharlal Nehru as the Prime Minister. The months leading up to the partition were marked by widespread unrest and strife resulting in an estimated death toll of one million. One of the largest migrations in human history took place as a result of which an estimated 10 million people crossed the border both ways. Those Muslims who could, mainly the upper and middle classes and many with family ties, migrated to Pakistan leaving India with a significant Muslim minority now constituting about 12 percent of the population. Nearly all Hindus and Sikhs migrated to India from East and West Pakistan. Numerous families were separated, and lost their properties. About 75 thousand women were believed to have been abducted, raped, and often forced to marry their abductors (Butalia 1998). Partition, therefore, was not a perfect solution, or an inevitable one. It resulted from the contradictions between various Indian social groups within the context of British policies that often played off and exaggerated cultural differences. Tensions and unrest continued in the months after India's independence, with Gandhi working hard to promote Hindu–Muslim unity within India. And in the midst of these efforts, Gandhi was assassinated on January 30, 1948, by a militant Hindu opposed to what was viewed as Gandhi's appeasement of Muslims.

After independence India adopted a Constitution that went into effect in 1950 and instituted a federal structure and parliamentary democracy modeled on Britain. In practice, the concern of the Indian government has been with maintaining unity leading to the increase of power at the central government level. Correspondingly, in the 52 years since India's independence numerous regional movements for autonomy and local power have emerged to challenge the center. There have been regular and frequent elections, and significant economic, industrial, and technological developments. However, poverty remains widespread, and education, health care, employment, and infrastructure are extremely inadequate, thereby undermining the capacity of people to fully participate in the democratic process. Formal liberal democracy, however, has provided a space for the political mobilization of people along class, caste, gender, community, and religious lines, adding to the complexity and uniqueness of contemporary Indian society.

CONCLUSION

Looking back over India's long recorded history of over 4,000 years, no one can characterize India as "unchanging," "traditional," or "backward," shaken into action by the arrival of the British. India was, and remains, a physically, politically, economically, and culturally dynamic and diverse society. The multiplicity of social forms results from centuries of interaction between local peoples and outsiders, as well as the interplay of peoples and groups within South Asia and later India. Culturally, a dominant Hindu tradition developed alongside numerous challenges and oppositions to it. And although some rulers may have patronized a certain religion over another, for the most part people of different faiths lived peacefully until the emergence of British colonial politics. Politically, there has been widespread regional and local autonomy, with central authority largely limited to military affairs and revenue generation. And political decentralization has not necessarily meant economic decline and chaos. In fact, Indian economic history shows several periods of economic prosperity, trade, and commerce, alongside economic inequalities well before the arrival of Europeans. It is clear, however, that British rule did introduce fundamental changes with lasting effects on post-independent India.

CHAPTER 3

Religions in India

In the late 1980s, when television started becoming more accessible and commercialized in India, two of the most popular shows were new productions of episodes from the great Hindu epics, **Ramayana** and **Mahabharata.** Each Sunday morning normal life came to a standstill, and streets emptied, as people gathered around TV sets to watch. For many, this popular rendering of the epics reinforced their faith and identity, whereas for others it was an entertaining pastime. This event illustrates the importance of religion as a significant part of spiritual as well as material existence in modern India. Non-Indians are often baffled by the coexistence of solemn rituals and worship with the colorful pageantry and spontaneity of hundreds of festivals celebrating various aspects of religions and seasons. Many North Americans and Europeans have turned to Eastern religions for spiritual fulfillment. And India is home to most major religions of the world, and also offers numerous avenues for spiritual expression. Hinduism and Buddhism arose in India, and Islam, Christianity, Sikhism, Jainism, and other smaller and tribal religions are also to be found.

As is apparent from the last chapter, no attempt to understand Indian society can ignore the ways in which religion has shaped Indian history, and continues to shape collective activities and individual lives in India. Some sociologists, such as Durkheim, elaborated on the integrative functions served by religious beliefs and practices. Others, such as Marx, focused on the use of religious beliefs by dominant groups to keep the masses from becoming aware of various forms of social inequality and oppression. In recent times we find more discussion of instances when religions have been used as the basis of intergroup conflict as well as liberation from oppression. In India, as in other parts of the world, religious beliefs and practices continue to be forces that integrate groups and communities, while simultaneously being the basis for the construction of boundaries that become implicated in intergroup conflict. Religious practices also form a significant basis for the formation of identities and finding meaning in one's life. As such, religion emerges as the basis of individual and collective action for spiritual renewal, and action to change and improve one's condition in life.

In this chapter, I will first summarize the historical and philosophical development of religions in India. An overview of religious diversity and changes will form the backdrop for the consideration of the role of religious thoughts and practices in contemporary politics and society in India.

HINDUISM

The religion now known as Hinduism has the largest number of adherents in India, accounting for about 82 percent of the population (over 800 million). Although some common philosophical principles can be traced to the first few centuries of the development of Hinduism, the religion is characterized by numerous texts and interpretations of beliefs and practices competing for legitimacy.

Hinduism is believed to have emerged around 2000 B.C. alongside the migration of Indo-Aryans into the Indus River Valley. There is no specific founder of Hinduism and no single scripture as the source of authority. The main beliefs are contained in the four main texts called the **Vedas,** compiled between 1500 and 900 B.C., and three supplemental texts compiled between 900 and 600 B.C. These orally-transmitted texts reflect the religious and social concerns of the Indo-Aryans who started out as nomadic and pastoral people, and eventually settled in agricultural communities over northern and central India by the sixth century B.C. Numerous deities are mentioned, including the strong and powerful Indra who has the ability to destroy evil and symbolizes the triumph of good over evil, and Agni or fire. They became an integral part of Vedic sacrificial rituals to defeat enemies as well as create, maintain, and stabilize cosmic and social order (Davis 1995: 7–11).

In the later *Vedas* we witness the emergence of a specific social category, called the Brahmans, specializing in interpreting and teaching the *Vedas* and conducting rituals. This marks the beginning of the development of what became institutionalized as the **caste system of stratification** (see Chapter 4). In the **Purusasukta hymn,** four main social categories emerge from the original man sacrificed, the Brahmans or priests from the mouth, the Kshatriyas or warriors from the arms, the Vaishyas or merchants from the loins, and Shudras or servants from the feet, symbolizing a hierarchical order from the highest to the lowest station in life (Davis 1995: 11).

In the course of the compilation of the *Vedas* there was a trend toward incorporating the plurality of gods and goddesses in Hinduism as part of a single divine principle, at some point also referred to as the Brahman or the omnipresent god. This monotheistic principle is physically represented by three main deities: **Brahma** the creator, **Vishnu** the preserver, and **Shiva** the destroyer and reproducer. Each god has a female aspect, and all other gods and goddesses are viewed as reincarnations of one of the three deities and their female counterparts.

In later centuries the *Vedas* came to be viewed as the classic sources of orthodox Hinduism, and the basis of epics such as the *Ramayana* and the *Mahabharata*, even as religious movements opposing Brahmanic rituals, hierarchy, and orthodoxy emerged. One of the supplementary Vedic texts, the *Upanishads*, contain the earlier elaborations of the key Hindu beliefs about the **transmigration of souls,** and the values of **dharma** and **karma.** According to this theory, a person goes through a continuous cycle of birth, death, and rebirth. As the human body is born, lives, and dies, the immortal soul passes from one living being to another. The nature of one's karma, or actions, broadly defined, in this life determine the status a person is reborn into. For the soul to pass on to a being of higher station, a person must lead a good, virtuous, and moral life, according to the dharma, or sacred duty expressed through a complex system of beliefs, rituals, and rules of conduct considered necessary to maintain the order of things. These rules relate to appropriate forms of social interaction with persons of different statuses, ritual practices, and ritual purity and pollution. For example, leading a ritually pure life includes following rules concerning whom to marry, appropriate diet, whom to associate with, and what occupations to engage in. These rules of conduct are too varied, complex, and everchanging to cover in detail here, but it is important to note that some apply to all who call themselves Hindus, whereas others vary by caste and other social categories. The aim of a Hindu is to live as good, virtuous, and moral a life as possible in order to be reborn in a higher position. The ultimate aim is to attain **moksha,** or spiritual salvation, that liberates us from the endless cycle of birth and death. One strategy to attain this state is through asceticism and renunciation of worldly life (Mathur 1992).

As Vedic traditions and Brahmanism came to be challenged by the rise and spread of Jainism and particularly Buddhism in the sixth century B.C., Hinduism underwent numerous changes and reformulation of its key beliefs over the next few centuries. This period, particularly during the Mauryan Empire in the fourth and third centuries B.C., is marked by the emergence of the great epics, the *Ramayana* and the *Mahabharata*, telling stories of wars in which the good and virtuous triumph over the evil. The *Mahabharata* tells the story of the conflict between the Pandavas and the Kauravas. It includes the **Bhagavad Gita,** popularly known as the *Gita,* in which Krishna, a reincarnation of Vishnu, relates to Arjuna, one of the Pandavas, the key beliefs and philosophies of Hinduism. In addition to instructing on the best ways to attain *moksha*, the *Gita* also allows for different paths to self-realization through the pursuit of *jnana* or knowledge, *bhakti* or devotion and love, and *karma* or work. Faith and spirituality, therefore, coexist with the practical pursuits of daily life. These literary texts, as well as the those later compiled as the **Puranas,** were passed on orally undergoing changes and varying interpretations. And by the seventh century A.D. Vishnu and Shiva emerged as supreme deities. However, between the fifth and seventh centuries, several goddesses also became important, both as consorts or wives of the male gods, such as Lakshmi, Parvati, and Sarawati, and as strong and independent deities, such as Durga and Kali (Davis 1995:21–27; Basham 1989:68–97).

Between A.D. 700 and 1200, under the patronage of Hindu kings, physical representations of these gods and goddesses were placed in large and elaborate temples, even as smaller temples and shrines in villages and people's homes allowed them direct access to the deities they worshipped. A particular form of worship, called **puja** or prayers, appeared, and replaced the earlier sacrificial rituals. The Brahmans, or priests, instituted themselves as the ones authorized to perform the *puja,* and mediate the ritual relationship between the deities and the worshippers (Davis 1995:27–29).

However, an alternative form of worship, called **Bhakti,** or devotion, also appeared in the South during the seventh century, allowing a devotee to express his or her faith through a close and direct emotional attachment to god, and by loving and serving god. Several poet–saints and communities of worshippers emerged within this tradition that spread to the north between the 12th and 17th centuries (Davis 1995:29–31). Bhakti poets expressed themselves in the local languages, and focused on different deities such as Shiva, Kali, and Krishna. However, they related to the deities in terms of a variety of personal human relationships, such as servant, friend, lover, mother, and so forth. This form of Hinduism, thus, became popular among the middle and lower castes and women. One of the most popular Bhakti poets of the 16th century is Mirabai, who left her traditional life married to a high-status Rajput prince to devote herself to god. Some devotees aimed to mainly attain inner peace and spiritual renewal, whereas others used their devotional pursuits to critique and improve prevailing social realities (Davis 1995:37–41). This movement spread alongside the arrival of Islam in India.

Later, with the establishment of British rule and expansion of Christian and other Western influences, movements for the reform of Hinduism emerged during the 19th century. Although varying in form and content, these movements critiqued several aspects of Hindu practices, such as those relating to the status of women, child marriage, rigid caste hierarchies, and elaborate rituals. The reformers invoked and recreated certain aspects of what they believed to be the classical and pure period of Hinduism when the *Vedas* were written and elaborated. This form of Hinduism became the basis of the dominant form of nationalism against the British. A pan-Indian culture became synonymous with a Hindu way of life. The nationalist movement for independence came to be viewed as a Hindu movement, leading some Muslim leaders to launch a movement for the creation of a separate Muslim state (see Chapter 2). And, as discussed in this chapter, and later in Chapter 8, religion has remained a significant element in post-independence politics in India.

Even as debates on the meaning and relevance of Hinduism in defining the essential nature of Indian nationhood continue, practices associated with Hinduism exhibit enormous diversity. A significant amount of religious activity goes on in homes, and in towns and villages. This popular Hinduism focuses on the worship of several gods and goddesses with whom devotees seek a close personal relationship. Although these practices often constitute a challenge to textual and Brahmanic interpretations of Hinduism, practitioners of popular Hinduism for the most part do not challenge the entire religious and social system. Most lower-status groups, such as women, and lower castes, except possibly the Dalits (or former untouchables), find a place in the system, and often seek to move up in the hierarchy, thereby accepting the legitimacy of the system. Women too find strength particularly through rituals associated with the goddesses, even though in reality they cannot often challenge the power of men in their family or society.

This popular, local, and domestic Hinduism is related to the public, textual, and pan-Indian Hinduism in a complex two-way relationship. Each selectively invokes and interprets elements from the other tradition and is continuously changing and reformulating. Although challenged and variously interpreted, Brahmanic Hinduism does present important normative standards, common themes, and principles for actual empirical practices. And in spite of the recent resurgence of Hindu nationalism and the attempts to define Hinduism in terms of a specific textual and ritual tradition, most Hindus continue to practice popular Hinduism in all its richness and diversity (Fuller 1992).

ISLAM

Founded in the early seventh century in the region around Mecca in what is now Saudi Arabia, Islam spread to India alongside the invasions of Arab, Persian, and Turkish armies over the next few centuries. Muslim rulers consolidated Islamic influence over most parts of northern and central India between A.D 700 and 1200. However, Hinduism continued to be widespread in India, and Muslims have emerged as the largest religious minority in India accounting for about 12 percent of the population. With over 100 million Muslims, India has one of the largest Muslim populations in the world. Islam in India ranges from an orthodox tradition to a more flexible and mystical **Sufi** tradition (Ahmed 1982).

Orthodox Islam focuses on a monotheistic belief in one supreme being, Allah, who is all-powerful and cannot be represented in any physical form on earth. Muhammad is believed to be the prophet who received revelations from Allah, and relates them to all who are believers. These revelations, in the form of ethical and spiritual principles for the conduct of daily life, are compiled in the **Qur'an.** The words and deeds of the Prophet Muhammad are compiled in the **Sunnah.** The Qur'an and the Sunnah form the basis of the **Sharia** or Islamic laws that provide guidelines for the conduct of personal and public life by Muslims. Practices based on the Sharia, however, vary cosiderably from one social context to another. All believers, regardless of their social and physical location, are included as part of a single community. A good Muslim must attempt to adhere to the "Five Pillars" of Islam. They are: acknowledging Allah as the only god, praying five times a day facing in the direction of Mecca, making charitable contributions, fasting during the holy month of Ramadan, and making a pilgrimage to Mecca at least once in a lifetime.

Islam, therefore, presents a striking contrast to Hinduism which centers around numerous gods and goddesses, and the hierarchical ordering of gods and people. Also, in contrast to Hinduism, public prayer in a mosque is important in Islam, and a strong distinction is made between believers and nonbelievers. There is a strong tradition in Islam to turn nonbelievers into believers through **jihad,** or righteous struggle now often interpreted as holy war.

Muslim rulers patronized Islam and displayed varying degrees of orthodoxy and flexibility in their policies. Although Islamic philosophy is very egalitarian and inclusive, Islamic rulers and clerics have usually accommodated local conditions. In India, Hindu rituals and practices were allowed so long as they did not challenge Islamic institutions. It was Sufism, however, that emerged as most flexible and least opposed to Hinduism. It was more successful in promoting acceptance of Islam in India, and gave Islam in India a distinctive indigenous quality (Davis 1995:31–37). Sufi saints and poets, usually ascetics leading a simple life, used poetry and music to spread Allah's words. Like the Bhakti poets, they promoted a close personal and direct relationship between believers and Allah, and did much to modify orthodox Islamic rituals and practices.

With the decline of the Mughal Empire and the consolidation of British rule, Indian Muslim elites initially stayed aloof, and resisted the influence of Western ideas, language, and culture. However, with the rise of Hindu reformism and nationalism, and the institution of English as the language of official business, a Muslim reform movement also emerged in order to connect Islamic beliefs with some aspects of modern science and technology. Later, as noted in Chapter 2, the Muslim League was formed in 1906, initially asking for separate electoral representation for Muslims in British India, and eventually demanding a separate state of Pakistan. Some issues relating to Islam in India after independence are discussed later in this chapter.

JAINISM AND BUDDHISM

Jainism and Buddhism emerged in India during the sixth century B.C. as a challenge to Brahamanic orthodoxy. Started by members of the Kshatriya or warrior caste in Magadha (present-day Bihar) during a time of increasing commercial and artistic endeavors, the two religions appealed most to members of lower-status castes. Jainism and Buddhism provided Vaishyas and Shudras spiritual fulfillment outside the rigid hierarchies of the Hindu caste system (Davis 1995:14–21).

Jainism was founded by Mahavira who was born in 599 B.C. He used the word "Jaina" to refer broadly to "conquering" of the senses through leading a pure and simple life as a means of attaining salvation and freedom from all bondage. In order to attain a release from the cycle of birth, death, and rebirth, the key to salvation, the Jains are expected to excercise self-restraint and several restrictions on food, rituals, and worldly and immoral activities. **Ahimsa,** or non-violence, is a key element of Jainism, and is linked to the belief that every living being has a soul, and that no life should be extinguished deliberately or inadvertantly. In practice, many sects and groups emerged within Jainism, ranging from less strict to more strict in adhering to the key beliefs. Whereas many Jains avoid meat, alcohol, stealing, lying, and violence, others renounce the world and lead an ascetic life. There are now two main Jain sects in India, the Svetambara who live mainly in western India, and the smaller Digambra sect mainly living in the South. In all, Jains currently number about four to five million.

Siddhartha Gautama, born in 566 B.C., founded Buddhism. He renounced an affluent princely family life when he was 29 years old, went on to lead an ascetic life, and attained enlightenment six years later. He took on the name *Buddha,* or one who has been awakened to true knowledge about life, believing that he had discovered the true cause of suffering in the world and the ways to overcome all suffering. Buddha identified the Four Noble Truths, namely, the world is full of suffering, this suffering is caused by human greed and worldly desires, attachment to worldly desires can be renounced, and renunciation can be attained by following the Eightfold Path. This Path includes eight "rights" or principles: the right views, right resolves, right speech, right conduct, right livelihood, right effort, right recollection, right meditation. Buddha also elaborated on how to conduct life according to the Eightfold Path. The eventual aim is to attain **Nirvana,** or a state of true emancipation through a release from the endless cycle of rebirth, and freedom from suffering.

The egalitarian philosophy of Buddhism allowed many women and men to become nuns and monks, and Buddhist monasteries became centers of education. Buddhism spread to many parts of central and northern India under royal patronage from the third to the seventh centuries A.D. After that the influence of Buddhism declined in India, but increased in Sri Lanka, China, Japan, and other parts of East and Southeast Asia, where it continues to be an important part of culture. There has also been an increase in the number of Buddhists in India during this century, particularly after independence when a significant number of Dalits in western India converted to Buddhism in order to escape their status as outcastes from Hinduism. The migration of Tibetans exiled from their homeland by Chinese occupation has also added to their numbers, and there are now approximately eight million Buddhists in India accounting for a little less than 1 percent of the total population.

SIKHISM

Sikhism emerged in India in the late 15th century when Muslim rule was being consolidated. This was also a time when Brahmanic orthodoxy was being reasserted. Criticisms of both Hindu and Muslim orthodoxy emerged as the Bhakti movement and the Sufi tradition became more popular in the North. A Bhakti poet, Kabir, raised in a Muslim weavers' community, synthesized Sufi, Bhakti, Buddhist, and other ideas to critique both Hinduism and Islam. He extolled the virtues of an all-powerful being who could not be described by humans, and stated that spirituality lay in devotion to the supreme being. Nanak, born in 1469 in a Hindu merchant family in Punjab, was deeply influenced by Kabir's ideas. He founded a new sect that developed over the next 200 years into the Sikh religion disctinct from both Hinduism and Islam. The key Sikh belief is in one god who is indescribable, all-powerful, and the embodiment of all knowledge and truth. The Sikhs reject worship of images and idols, and spiritual faith is expressed through devotion, congregational worship, living honestly, and caring for others. Islamic influence on Sikhism is reflected in its strong monotheism, and opposition to the caste system and idol worship. Sikhism, however, retains the ideas of karma and rebirth, and everyday life and rituals show significant Hindu influence. An essentially egalitarian message was spread by a guru, or religious teacher, and Nanak is the first Sikh guru (McLeod 1989:16–31, 48–59). He was followed by nine more gurus in succession, until the last guru, Gobind Singh, proclaimed in the late 17th century that henceforth the teachings of the first five gurus compiled in the **Adi Granth,** the Sikh holy book, would serve as the guru.

Although the Sikhs borrowed key Islamic spiritual ideas, they came into increasing conflict with Mughal rulers, and were often persecuted. Gobind Singh, in 1699, further distinguished the Sikh religion from others by creating the **Khalsa** order, or the community of the pure ones, committed to the defense of their faith. Five physical symbols became the key to the Sikh identity and lifestyle, known as the five "K"s: the *kes*, or uncut hair, symbolizing faith in god and noninterference in the natural order; the *kirpan*, or small dagger, symbolizing defense of the truth and what is right; the *kanga*, or comb, as a symbol of cleanliness and orderliness; the *kara*, or steel bangle, as a symbol of eternity, strength, and purity; and the *kachh*, or loose shorts, symbolizing alertness, purity, and modesty. These symbols emerged out of practical considerations while the Sikhs defended the faith particularly against persecution by Muslim rulers. Most Sikhs today exhibit varying degrees of adherence to Sikh principles and the five "k"s, many have cut their hair and a few choose to be formally initiated into the Khalsa order. Sikhs are most recognizable today by their often colorful turbans, worn on their heads to manage their long hair, and their beards.

The Sikhs emerged as strong fighters and maintained an independent Sikh kingdom in the Punjab which was the strongest under Ranjit Singh in the early 19th century. They were eventually subdued by the British in the 1840s, becoming the last key region to fall to the British in India. Their military skills resulted in their induction into the British Indian army, and they also became successful agriculturalists. This trend has remained strong in post-independence India, although there has been some diversification among them (McLeod 1989; Singh 1963, 1977). Sikhs now constitute about 2 percent, or approximately 20 million, of the Indian population. As discussed in Chapter 8, many Sikhs feel persecuted as a minority, and have become involved in political tensions in India in recent decades.

OTHER SMALLER RELIGIONS

Several other religions are also practiced in India, including tribal religions, Christianity, Zoroastrianism, and Judaism. Among many of the more islolated tribal groups in India, spiritual life centers around the forces of nature, although practices vary tremendously from one group to another. As they become less isolated, tribal groups face pressures to convert to the other dominant mainstream religions, and a significant proportion have converted to Christianity. There are now about 22 million Christians from various denominations in India. St. Thomas, the apostle, is believed to have first introduced Christianity to India in the first century A.D., but Christianity spread mainly after the arrival of Vasco da Gama in 1498, and especially St. Francis Xavier in 1542, in Goa. Christians have had the most success in incorporating members of tribal groups and the

Dalits into their fold. The highest proportion of Christians in India is in the South, particularly in the state of Kerala. However, Christian missions and educational institutions are to be found all over India.

A small group of about 1,000,00 Parsis also live in western India, mostly in and around Bombay (now Mumbai). They follow Zoroastrianism, a religion founded in Persia in the sixth century B.C. The Parsis brought the religion with them when they migrated to India in the eighth century A.D. following the Arab conquest of Iran. The religion centers on the conflict between good and evil, and the victory of good over evil through faith in the god Ahura Mazda, or the "Wise Lord" symbolized by fire. Although small in number, Parsis have played a pioneering role in trade and industry, as well as in technological and educational developments in India. India's largest industrial corporation, the Tata Group, was founded by Parsis. Two very small groups of Jews, now numbering only about 5,000, live in India. The Jews of Kochi in Kerala claim to have arrived in 587 B.C. Another group is the Marathi-speaking group, the Bene Israel or Children of Israel.

RELIGION, NATIONALISM, AND POLITICS

The emergence and development of religions in India are, therefore, closely associated with its political and social history. As is clear from Chapter 2, religious ideas and interpretations played an important role in defining the nature of the nationalist movement for independence from Britain. And India's religious diversity has taken on new forms in the political and cultural processes since independence.

The dominant form of nationalism that emerged in India in the late 19th century was constructed and propagated by Hindu intellectuals who formed the leadership of the Indian National Congress. They accepted the European definition of a **nation–state** based on the correspondence between a strong state and a group of people sharing a unique cultural identity. Given the numerous non-Hindu religions in India, and the diversity within Hinduism, these leaders focused on Hinduism as a tolerant and humane religion with the capacity to include varying viewpoints. Indian nationalist leaders also argued that Indian national identity was based on a common humanity and spirituality that transcends any specific beliefs and practices.

This interpretation of Indian culture was incorporated into the official state ideology of **secularism** after independence. Although in the North American context secularism is defined as a process whereby religious ideas and practices have little influence on other aspects of social life, the term has acquired a different and varied practical connotation in India. Secularism in India is interpreted as maintaining an equal distance from all religions, denying the dominance of any particular religion, allowing freedom to practice any religion, assuming a neutral stance with respect to religion, and not interfering in the internal affairs of any religion (Embree 1990; Madan 1992). The Indian National Congress that ruled in India under Nehru for the first 17 years after independence attempted to conduct itself according to this view of secularism. Many Muslim traders, professionals, and industrialists migrated to Pakistan at the time of independence, leaving a significant section of economically depressed and demoralized Muslims. They, for the most part, supported the Congress and its official ideology of secularism as the best they could hope for in a Hindu-majority country.

In reality, however, the Indian government, mostly Congress led until recently, has constantly been trying to balance and accommodate the competing demands of different religions and groups within them. Even as the state has asserted that it maintains neutrality and equal distance from all groups, it has been increasingly involved in religious affairs. For instance, the government resolved to grant equality to all its citizens under a **Uniform Civil Code** (UCC). However, it made allowances for the protection of certain customary or personal laws relating to property, marriage, education, and other issues deemed by some religious leaders as sanctioned by their respective religious beliefs. Hence, whereas some sections of Hindu customary laws were modified and incorporated into the Uniform Civil Code, exceptions were made in the case of minority religions, particularly Islam and Christianity. This has created an ongoing tension between some sections of the Hindus and minority religions. Many Hindus argue that religious minorities are accorded too much autonomy thereby undermining Indian unity, whereas many minorities charge that the Uniform Civil Code reflects Hindu social and religious practices, and resist its institution as an interference in the internal affairs of their religion.

Since the late 1960s, when the Congress started facing challenges to its authority at the central and state levels, there was also a reemergence of political action along religious and ethnic lines, known in India as **communalism.** The Congress and other political parties have increasingly used religion and caste as the basis for political mobilization (see Chapters 8 and 4). This process has taken place alongside the resurgence of a Hindu nationalist ideology known as **Hindutva.**

The idea of India as a nation based on Hinduism as both a religion and cultural basis of Indian civilization was first explicitly constructed in the 1920s. In the view of some Hindus, India is more appropriately termed "Hindustan" or the Land of the Hindus, stretching from the Indus River to the seas surrounding the Deccan Peninsula. Those religious traditions that developed on this land, including Hinduism, Jainism, Buddhism, and Sikhism, are viewed as part of Hindustan. However, Islam and Christianity originated outside Hindustan in this view, but can be incorporated into Hindustan through assimilation, acceptance of Hinduism as the basis of the Indian nation, and exhibiting loyalty to the nation. Hinduism is interpreted as a unified and homogeneous cultural and religious system as distinct to, say, Islam. In the formulation of the Hindutva ideology, the diversities within Hinduism are downplayed or ignored, as are the severe critiques of Hindu orthodoxy and ritual practices contained in Jainism, Buddhism, Sikhism, some forms of popular Hinduism, and the Dalit and anti-caste movements. Also ignored is the cross-fertilization of various ideas among Hinduism, Islam, and other religious traditions over the centuries (Patnaik and Chalam 1996).

This view is propagated by the Vishwa Hindu Parishad (VHP), or World Hindu Council, and the Rashtriya Swayamsevak Sangh (RSS), both conservative and militant Hindu organizations. In electoral politics, the Jana Sangh and later the Bharatiya Janata Party (BJP), have promoted the notion of India as a strong nation based on the Hindu way of life. Support for Hindutva comes mainly from the urban unemployed and non-Dalit rural poor. The rise in popularity of right-wing Hindu nationalism and the appeal of religious and ethnic loyalties has emerged alongside the decline in support for the Congress and the economic crises since the 1970s. And during the 1980s and 1990s, communal politics have become increasingly significant in India, as is evident particularly in the cases of Punjab and Kashmir discussed in Chapter 8.

However, the relations between Hindus and Muslims in India have emerged as the most significant form of communalism in India in the last 15 years. The debate over competing ideologies of India as a secular nation or a Hindu nation is reflected in two events. The first is the controversy surrounding the Muslim woman, Shah Bano, who sought alimony from her ex-husband under the Indian Civil Code in 1984. Although the case is discussed in detail in Chapter 6, what is significant here is that while the Indian Supreme Court upheld Shah Bano's claim, many orthodox Muslim groups were outraged. The Government of India passed the Muslim Women's Bill in Parliament in 1986, upholding Muslim Personal Law and overturning the Supreme Court decision. Many Hindu nationalists as well as secular groups and women's groups in India viewed the Bill as an appeasement of Muslims for electoral gain, a breach of secularism, and/or a violation of women's rights.

The debate over the Shah Bano case took place within the context of a growing movement among some Hindu nationalist groups, particularly the VHP, for reclaiming a piece of land on which a mosque stood to build a Hindu temple in the town of Ayodhya. Ayodhya is believed by many Hindus to be the birthplace of the Hindu god Ram. They believe that a Hindu temple stood on this piece of land until 1528 when Babur, the founder of the Mughal Empire, demolished it to build a Muslim mosque, known as Babri Masjid. As a complex court case continued, the Hindu nationalists claimed that this was a religious matter and hence not something that could be decided upon by the courts. And when the Indian government intervened to pass the Muslim Women's Bill in 1986, the BJP, a political party participating in electoral politics, started openly supporting the VHP movement to build a Hindu temple. Matters escalated when on December 6, 1992, a large number of Hindus gathered at Ayodhya and demolished the mosque. This embarrassed the BJP government then in power in the state of Uttar Pradesh (where Ayodhya is located) as well as the central government as no one overtly wanted to hurt Muslim sentiments. This event was followed by weeks of some of the worst anti-Muslim riots in India since independence (Varshney 1993).

Somewhat sobered by this turn of events, the BJP tempered its rhetoric in support of building a temple. Also, it has had to moderate its demands for Hindutva in order to appeal to a broader segment of the Indian population if it is to increase its support base. Although most support of the BJP comes from sections in northern, eastern, and western India, the BJP has managed to win more seats in successive elections and headed a coalition government in India during 1998–99. The issue of a temple at Ayodhya is still not settled, however. Many right-wing militant Hindu groups and self-styled defenders of the faith have become more active, with attacks on Christians causing the most alarm in recent months.

Meanwhile, the debate on secularism and its relevance in India continues. Some, such as Madan (1992), argue that secularism is a Western concept that does not resonate with the social and cultural realities in India. This is so because religion remains an integral part of people's lives, and affects many other facets of societal life. It is, therefore, difficult to maintain religious neutrality. Others, such as Mushirul Hasan (1996), however, believe that promoting and maintaining a genuine commitment to secularism is the only hope for peace and tolerance in a culturally diverse society such as India. This secularism, they argue, needs to be reflected both at the state level in formal political institutions and at the local community level.

CONCLUSION

It is clear from this chapter and others that religion is an enormously significant part of cultural, political, and social life in India. Religious life has historically been closely related to political processes, and India's religious variety continues to be at the center of political debates in India. As a result, religion has been implicated in numerous conflicts and tensions in India. However, religion has also been an important source of identity and integration. For the most part, people practice their religions in private, express their religiosity in numerous ways, participate in religious festivals with great enthusiasm, and continue to travel to visit various holy sites. Religion continues to be an important outlet for self-expression as in most other parts of the world.

CHAPTER 4

Social Stratification

While India celebrated 50 years of independence from Britain in the summer of 1997, it also elected scholar, diplomat, and political leader Dr. K. R. Narayanan as its president. The election of the president usually does not arouse much public interest in India as the position is mainly ceremonial; real political power resides with the prime minister who is the head of the government under India's parliamentary system modeled on Great Britain. Dr. Narayanan's appointment as head of state, however, marks the first time a person from one of India's lowest castes, defined earlier as untouchable and now referred to as Dalits, has risen to such high office. For many, this event symbolizes the progress made by the lower-status castes in India, and they also note that Dr. Narayanan reached this position on the basis of merit and distinguished service to the nation. Others, however, point out that this event cannot overshadow the severe disadvantages faced by millions of lower castes and tribal groups who are disproportionately among India's poor and illiterate.

Historically, caste in India is one of the main dimensions along which people in India are socially differentiated along with class, religion, region, tribe, gender, and language. Some form of differentiation exists in all human societies, but these differences and diversities become problematic when one or more of these dimensions overlap and become the basis of systematic ranking and unequal access to valued resources, such as wealth, income, power, and prestige. Systems of **social stratification** may be normatively "closed" or "open." A **closed system of stratification** is one in which a person's social status is conferred by birth, is very difficult to change, and there are limits on interaction with persons of another social status. Alternatively, in an **open system of stratification** a person's social status is ideally based on individual talent and ability, making it possible to move up or down in social rank.

The **caste system** in India, with its normative classification of people into four hierarchically ranked occupational castes, numerous occupationally specialized sub-castes, hereditary membership in castes, and access to wealth, power, and privilege on the basis of caste, is viewed as the main example of a closed system of stratification. Analysis of social stratification in India has, appropriately, focused on the caste system and variations within the system. Until recently, however, most analysts viewed caste in India as rigid and unchanging. And when change was discussed, focus was on whether, and the extent to which, it would give way to class as the basis of stratification.

A **class system of stratification** is viewed as an example of an open system of stratification in which economic status, based on ownership or nonownership of wealth and property or on occupation and skill level, is the basis of social rank. In theory, therefore, it is possible to change one's economic and social status, although in practice individuals may face significant advantages or disadvantages as a result of inherited class position, race, ethnicity, and gender, such as in the United States. More technologically developed and industrialized societies, like the United States, however, are said to exemplify the class system of stratification. And there is an expectation that as India becomes more industrialized and modernized along Western lines, class would become a more important indicator of social rank than caste.

As I will elaborate in this chapter, however, the situation in India is much more complex and dynamic than has been assumed. Economic class position is an important indicator of social status in India today, but it was important in the past also. However, in the past, economic position overlapped much more closely with caste ranking than at present, and caste ranking was very closely related to the nature of one's occupation. The caste system was not as inflexible in the past as is often assumed. There were regional variations in ranking, many individuals and groups did change their caste position, and there were numerous disputes over how ranks were assigned, as well as challenges to the legitimacy of caste hierarchies. But caste continues to be an important element in the social, economic, and political life of modern India, although in a different form than in the past.

CASTE IN INDIA

In principle, the caste system is composed of the fourfold **varna** scheme in which the **Brahmans,** usually priests and scholars, are at the top. They are followed, in order, by the **Kshatriyas,** or political rulers and soldiers, the **Vaishyas,** or merchants, and the **Shudras,** who are usually laborers, peasants, artisans, and servants. At the bottom are those considered **untouchable** who perform occupations that are considered unclean and polluting, such as scavenging and skinning dead animals and are, there-fore, defined as the outcastes. Each varna is divided into numerous sub-castes, or **jatis.** Each jati is composed of a group deriving its livelihood primarily from a specific occupation. People become members of a caste through birth and acquire appropriate occupations as a result. The hereditary occupational specialization and hierarchical ranking of occu-pations is, in theory, maintained through an elaborate ritual system regu-lating the nature of social interaction between the jatis (Ghurye 1991 [1969]; Bougle 1991 [1958]). Vedic texts, compiled, legitimized, and inter-preted by the Brahmans, provide the rationale for the hierarchical classi-fication and the rituals governing social behavior. Numerous ethnogra-phies of villages in India during the 1950s and 1960s documented the structure and functioning of caste. They described caste hierarchies as fairly stable and rigid. Recent studies, however, indicate that the Brah-manic interpretation of caste was more of a theoretical ideal over much of India until the arrival and consolidation of British rule after 1750 (Fuller 1996; Srinivas 1996; Gupta 1991 a and b). Also, in the late 19th century, the British started taking a census of the local population in India. They recorded what they believed was a legitimate and inflexible system based largely on the Brahmanic interpretation. British policies contributed to making caste more institutionalized and inflexible, and the Brahmanical position more dominant. In reality, Brahmanism was never unchallenged, and actual practices varied considerably through time, and in different parts of the country.

Explanations of caste in India tend to focus on its religious and rit-ual legitimation as part of Hinduism. Indeed there were, and still are, rules prescribing appropriate occupational pursuits, appropriate behav-ior within and between castes, as well as rules concerning marriage. For example, sharing certain kinds of food, and on certain occasions, with lower castes, and even touching someone from a lower caste, are consid-ered polluting. Members of higher castes engage in purification rituals to cleanse themselves and their homes. Residential segregation and limits on movement by members of lower castes in certain parts of the village, or certain temples, are also means to ensure social and physical distance between castes. However, it is important to note that since about 600 B.C. higher or lower ritual status has been associated with the nature of the occupation. Also, access to material resources and rewards was attached to occupational status. And after A.D. 300, it became increasingly possible to change ones occupation, and hence caste status. For example, Brah-mans, Kshatriyas, Vaishyas, and even Shudras, acquired land or varying degrees of rights to land by performing services associated with their re-spective caste. As a result, numerous agricultural castes emerged, al-though Brahmans and Kshatriyas tended to be the main landowners in parts of the country where they were present in larger numbers. Key rit-ual functions, though, were performed by the Brahmans. The artisan castes were more likely to engage in their traditional occupations as weavers, potters, blacksmiths, and so on. Depending on the village and region, occupations such as trade and enterprise, military service, agricultural work, and some artisan trades, were performed by members of more than one caste.

There is evidence of numerous instances of castes changing their ritual status through moving to another area and acquiring new occupations and economic and political power. Through a process termed **sanskritization,** a low caste, tribe, or other group takes on the customs, rituals, beliefs, ideology, and style of life of a high caste (Srinivas 1991 [1989]). However, higher-ritual status did not always correspond with greater economic or political power. In Punjab, for example, Jats, Ahirs, and Rajputs, originally Shudras or Kshatriyas, had greater military power and land rights than the Brahmans.

Moreover, the number and distribution of castes vary in different parts of India. According to the 1931 census, the last time a detailed caste census was taken, about 6.4 percent of the Hindu population was Brahman, 3.7 percent Rajputs, the main Kshatriya group, and 2.7 percent Vaishyas. The Brahmans and Kshatriyas were more concentrated in the northern and central parts of India, particularly the Ganga Valley, and it is here that the varna-based hierarchy was most in evidence. A strong distinction separated the upper three castes from the Shudras and the untouchables, with the latter being denied education, limited to manual and service occupations, and mistreated. In the South, only about 3 to 4 percent of the Hindus were Brahmans, and very few were Kshatriyas and Vaishyas. Although a strong ritual and social distance separated the highest from the lowest castes, the dominant castes controlling land were mainly Shudras. In practice, therefore, there have been more accommodation and coexistence between the Brahmans and the Shudras in the South, many of whom have been able to attain the status of "clean" Shudras to match their economic status (Frankel 1989:5–7).

Furthermore, the lower castes did not always accept the Brahmanic myths explaining their lower status, and developed their own myths in which they expressed hostility toward the Brahman claims to superiority. They often explained their lower status as a result of the economic and political power and greed of the upper castes rather than as preordained (Gupta 1991b:110–41). Also, as the discussion of religions in India shows, several religious movements, such as Bhakti, Buddhism, Jainism, and Sikhism, explicitly challenged the legitimacy of the caste system. These as well as other movements characterized by what Rao (1989:28) calls "a spirit of reform, dissent and protest," countered the hierarchy and group orientation related to caste with egalitarian values and individual expression. For example, the Satnamis emerged in the early 19th century in the Chattisgarh region of Madhya Pradesh in central India, and rejected the gods, goddesses, and rituals legitimized by the Brahmans. They were from the Chamar group, defined as untouchable by the Brahmans. Their founder, Ghasidas, developed a faith based on a belief in a formless god termed Satnam, or true name. They rejected the Brahmanical caste order, but over the next 100 years developed their own hierarchical organization rationalized through myths, rituals, and practices associated with the founder and his family and descendents. Although they developed certain castelike features, the Satnamis succeeded in the 1920s in persuading the British not to include them as untouchables on the list of castes being compiled by the British (Dube 1998).

Although caste has for centuries been important in India, there is no single principle accepted by all groups as the basis of assigning rank all over the country. Overall, several elements of the system remain, particularly in rural India, while it has undergone significant changes during this century, particularly after independence.

Caste in India since Independence

Anthropologist Adrian Mayer observed the social structure of the village of Ramkheri in central India in 1954, and visited it several times until 1992 (Mayer 1996). In 1954 Mayer documented an elaborate caste system at the center of the village social structure. There were 25 sub-castes or jatis and two Muslim groups divided broadly into five categories somewhat like the varna scheme, with Brahmans at the top, several agricultural, trading, and artisan castes in the middle, and the weaver, tanner, and sweeper at the bottom. Within each larger category, however, were several jatis of relatively equal rank, each with a distinct occupation and each practiced **endogamy,** or marriage within the caste group. The ranking was based on beliefs about purity and pollution expressed through practices relating to social interaction among the groups. For example, members of a jati that considered itself to be superior to another, did not give or take food from the jati they considered lower in status. If members of a jati took food from members of another jati, then the takers of food were viewed to be of equal or lower status than the food-givers. There were also rules relating to how the food was cooked, as well as the context within which food was shared, for instance as part of weddings or funerals.

By 1992, Mayer observed considerable change in, and relaxation of, rules concerning food sharing. There was more sharing between members of the middle and upper castes, but those in the lowest castes continued to eat separately from the rest. Rituals concerning food appear to be stricter on ceremonial occasions. There is a lot more eating at local and nearby restaurants and teashops, particularly among men. And here, caste distinctions are less likely to be made.

There was a significant change in the occupational pursuits among men from 1954 to 1992. Earlier, most men were engaged in their traditional caste-related occupations, such as blacksmithing, tanning, pottery making. Farming was pursued by traditional agriculturists and others whose traditional occupations had declined. By 1992, most Ramkheri natives had taken up newer occupations that had emerged in the village or in nearby towns, such as government jobs, teaching, retail and services, and machine repair. There was, however, still some caste-based prejudice and ritual ranking in the village even when individuals did not pursue traditional caste occupations. Wealth and power in the village was now less associated with caste than before, and landownership had become more diversified. Benefits from the newer occupations, however, had gone mainly to the middle and upper castes. Electoral politics had by now made political power more diversified. In the sphere of marriage and family relations, caste endogamy continues to be the norm, and has become a more important indicator of caste status.

Other recent studies suggest similar varied trends in the meaning and significance of caste in rural India, where about 75 percent of Indians continue to reside. There is a definite relaxation in ideas of purity and pollution in inter-caste relations, and more meat eating and consumption of alcohol. But this relaxation is more observable in public settings, such as restaurants, and in urban areas. Inside the homes and on ceremonial occasions, purification rituals relating to caste status are still observed. Caste endogamy is still widespread, although there is a somewhat broader range of jatis of relatively similar status within which marriage is arranged. There is a significant change in occupational specialization by caste, mostly because of a decline in traditional occupations and the rise of industrialization and related modern occupations. There has been a corresponding decline in an institution of patron-client relations known as the **jajmani system,** in which castes performing specialized occupations exchanged goods and services within the village. However, those still engaged in the traditional skills and trades continue to be mainly from the caste specializing in that occupation. Movement out of the traditional occupations has been much slower among the lower castes, and the middle and upper castes have more resources to enable them to take advantage of new opportunities (Karanth 1996). In many rural areas, there is still evidence of lower castes engaging in sanskritization to raise their status.

In urban areas, where about 25 percent of Indians reside, caste is a less significant part of daily life than in rural areas. But its significance varies by social class and occupation. Among the urban middle-class professionals, in particular, caste is not overtly discussed, and is for the most part not the main basis for status except when it comes to marital arrangements. Even then, caste considerations are often modified by factors such as education, occupation, and income, as well as religion and language (Beteille 1996).

Rituals associated with the purity of the home and food preparation are the preserve of women, and women traditionally also played an important role in the jajmani system of exchange relations between castes. To the extent that these relations are still prevalent, women continue to play a significant role in maintaining caste distinctions. There is also greater emphasis on female purity, and more restrictions on women than men in issues relating to marriage and sexuality. This gender-based distinction is more prevalent among the upper castes than among the lower castes, and is also expressed through more control among upper castes on women's productive labor outside the household. A woman's status is tied to the status of the male. In many instances, it is desirable for a woman to marry a man of equal- or higher-status caste, but a man may not marry a woman of a higher caste. However, men of a higher caste have easier sexual access to women of a lower caste. Caste, then, emerges as a medium through which asymmetrical gender relations are expressed (Dube 1996).

Although discrimination on the basis of caste has been outlawed in India, caste has assumed an important role in electoral politics. Caste affiliation has become an important basis for mobilization of support during elections. Caste has also become a means for competing for access to valued resources in modern India, such as educational opportunities, new occupations, and improvement in life chances. This trend is connected to India's preferential policies, similar to affirmative action in America, for members of historically disadvanteged lower castes. These are discussed later in this chapter.

Caste and Religion

Traditionally, the caste system of stratification in India was legitimized through classical Hindu religious texts, especially as interpreted by Brahmans. Through the introduction of English legal, administrative, economic, and educational institutions, the British undermined Brahmanic legitimization of economic and social hierarchies associated with caste, even though they solidified the power of many of the local dominant groups in many areas and hardened caste boundaries. This process has continued during the 20th century, with a significant trend toward dissociation of caste from Hinduism, although the relationship between caste and Hinduism remains a complex one.

To the extent that caste-based rituals are practiced, these practices take place mainly among the Hindus, the majority religion in India. Many in India continue to see caste as an essential part of Hinduism. This was a primary reason for the conversion to Buddhism of many who were defined as untouchables during the 1950s under the leadership of B. R. Ambedkar. Conversion to Buddhism was believed to be the only means of emancipation from the injustices associated with the caste system. Those termed untouchables now refer to themselves as **Dalit,** or the oppressed people, and the term is used to denote both pride in their community as well as resistance to exploitation. Sometimes the oppressed Shudra castes and tribal groups also refer to themselves as Dalit. Many who are active in the Dalit movements against social and economic injustice explicitly reject being defined as Hindu. They seek, instead, to increase knowledge and consciousness about their distinct cultural heritage and religious beliefs and practices (e.g., Ilaiah 1996, 1997).

However, in earlier periods, and even during this century, various religious movements have sought to rid Hinduism of caste. The reform movements during the 19th century, and Gandhian philosophy during this century, attempted to eliminate practices that express hierarchy and inequality, usually through caste. Ironically, those groups now organizing to promote the idea of India as a Hindu nation (see Chapter 3) are also downplaying the connection between caste and Hinduism in order to gain a larger following, even as they use caste categories to generate support. Overall, Hinduism is increasingly being delinked from any necessary connection with caste, although many members of minority religions and Dalits do not always believe this to be the case (Jayaram 1996).

That there is no necessary connection between caste and Hinduism is also reflected in the status differences within other Indian religions that are often expressed in caste-like terms but without being legitimized by Brahmanism. Although Muslim, Sikh, and Christian leaders deny the existence of caste in those religions, scholars provide evidence of some remnants of caste practices among those who converted from Hinduism, or those influenced by the wider Hindu society in the regions in which they lived as minorities (Fuller 1991; Bhatty 1996; Tharamangalam 1996; Vatuk 1996).

In India and elsewhere, a distinction is made between Muslims who converted to Islam earlier, and those who converted later, with the former being granted a higher status. In India, there is a further distinction made between the **Ashrafs,** or descendents of Muslims of foreign origin, and **non-Ashrafs,** or those who converted to Islam as a consequence of Muslim rule in India. Within each category Bhatty (1996) observed several hierarchically ranked castes in a village in North Central India. Differences among the castes were expressed through rituals relating to purity and impurity, hereditary occupations, and limits on social interaction. Although by the 1980s there was some loosening and flexibility in these rules, marriage was still largely endogamous. Among the non-Ashrafs there was some evidence of a process like sanskritization especially if they acquired land, whereas among the Ashrafs, there was more evidence of **westernization** as a result of access to modern occupations. Similar trends have been observed among Muslims elsewhere in India (see e.g., Ahmed 1991 [1973]; Vatuk 1996) although there is also a tendency to deny that the status differences among Muslims are akin to caste because of the egalitarian Islamic philosophy.

As a result of the influence of converts and the surrounding social, economic, and political environment, caste differences are also to be found among Christians, particularly in rural areas (Tharamangalam 1996). In the southern Indian state of Kerala, where the largest proportion of Christians in India live, Syrian Christians are considered to be of the highest status. They are believed to be the earliest converts and from the Brahman caste. Many of the later converts, particularly from the 19th century onward, are from the lower castes, Dalits and tribal groups, both in Kerala and in other parts of India. At present, approximately 50 percent of Christians in India are from among the Dalits, about 25 percent from the middle and upper castes, and the rest from tribal and other groups. In villages and small towns in particular, caste practices can still be observed, such as endogamy, regulation of social interaction, and even separate congregations for Dalit Christians.

However, relations between the different groups among Christians are more flexible than among many Hindu castes, and there is more of a correlation of status difference with economic factors. In recent decades there have also been movements among Dalit Christians to protest discrimination within the church and to improve their position. Some have formed separate Dalit churches, and some have even converted back to Hinduism and claimed lower-caste status that would then make them eligible for preferential state policies. Inequalities associated with caste are not visible to the same extent among tribal converts to Christianity. A caste hierarchy did not exist among tribal groups and, once converted, many experienced rapid educational and economic improvements.

Sikhism sought to provide a spiritual outlet for people without the hierarchical ordering of people in terms of caste. However, some elements of caste did filter into Sikh social structure although in a different form than among Hindus. The two dominant castes among the Sikhs are the **Jats** and the **Khatris.** The Jats, originally believed to be a tribal group, emerged as the dominant agricultural group among the Sikhs. The Khatris, originally from the Kshatriya caste, are predominantly traders and entrepreneurs, and have traditionally lived mainly in urban areas. Both claim to be the highest caste among Sikhs. There are also many artisan castes among the Sikhs and also Dalits, earlier known as **mazhabi** Sikhs. As among the Hindus, caste distinctions are more visible in rural areas, especially in residential patterns. Marriages are also more likely to be arranged within the castes. However, there has been more occupational diversification among all the Sikh castes. But caste remains an important marker of identity, and a basis of mobilization for political activities.

Caste, Political Action, and Policies

The nature and significance of caste in India have been fundamentally affected by various efforts to overcome the inequalities and injustices associated with caste. These include movements to gain equality for the lower castes, and government measures in pre- and post-independence India.

In the Census of India started by the British in the late 19th century, those engaging in what the Brahmans viewed as unclean tasks were termed "untouchables." During the nationalist movement, Gandhi started using the term "Harijans," or god's people, as a more positive term of reference, even though many lower caste members consider the term patronizing. In 1935, the British Government of India came up with a list of 400 groups considered untouchable, as well as many tribal groups, that would be accorded special privileges in order to overcome deprivation and discrimination. Those groups included on this list came to be termed **Scheduled Castes** and **Scheduled Tribes.** In the 1970s, however, many leaders of castes considered untouchable started calling themselves Dalits.

Although historically there have been several challenges to orthodox Hinduism and caste hierarchy, these movements became more widespread during the last two centuries. The anti-caste Dalit movement has its roots in the work of Jyotirao Phule in the mid-19th century. Phule started a movement for education and upliftment of women, Shudras, and Dalits, and the movement spread to many parts of India. He also worked to abolish untouchability, getting rid of restrictions on entry into temples, and finding a place for Dalits within Hinduism. After 1910, however, Dalit leaders started focusing more on distancing themsleves from Hinduism, as part of an effort to gain a separate electorate for Dalits just like the one for Muslims. But the leadership of the Indian National Congress, especially Gandhi, attempted to incorporate Dalits as part of reformed Hinduism (Omvedt 1996:336–38; Suresh 1996:358–62).

During the 1920s and 1930s a Dalit from the Mahar caste in Maharashtra in western India, B. R. Ambedkar, emerged as a leader of the Dalits. He campaigned for greater rights for Dalits in British India, and later within an independent India. Ambedkar and Gandhi, however, disagreed on the reasons for the subordinate status of Dalits, and measures to improve their status. Gandhi believed untouchability to be a moral issue that could be abolished through goodwill and change of heart among the upper-caste Hindus. Ambedkar, though, believed that the subordination of Dalits was primarily economic and political, and could only be overcome by changing the social structure through legal, political, and educational means. As part of constitutional guarantees after independence, Ambedkar agreed to the reservation of a certain percentage of seats in elections for the Dalits, as well as laws abolishing untouchability, and the granting of various rights to Dalits and other disadvantaged groups as detailed below. By the mid-1950s, however, Ambedkar became disillusioned with the lack of implementation of the measures, resigned from the government, and started mobilizing the Dalits to seek rights. In 1956, he led approximately six million Dalits, mainly from the Mahar caste, into converting to Buddhism as a means of escaping the social stigma of untouchability within the Hindu caste system (Omvedt 1996:338–42; Suresh 1996:362–68).

During the 1970s, the Dalit Panthers movement, inspired by the Black Panthers in the United States, emerged among the younger generation of Dalits alongside other social movements in India. They were angered and frustrated at the failure of implementation of policies and continuing acts of violence against Dalits by upper-caste Hindus in many parts of rural India in particular. Several Dalit groups are now active in many parts of the country, and in the late 1970s a Dalit-based political party, the Bahujan Samaj Party (BSP), emerged in northern India. The BSP has participated in elections and has recently increased its support, and even briefly gained power in the state of Uttar Pradesh, ironically with the support of the BJP which is a more conservative Hindu-based party.

State Policies to Eliminate Caste Inequalities

As part of the constitutional promise of equality and freedom and elimination of inequalities associated with lower-caste and untouchable status, the Government of India has instituted preferential policies, similar to what is known as affirmative action in the United States. For those groups classified as eligible for preferential treatment there is reservation of seats in legislatures, in government jobs, in public sector enterprises, and in state-supervised educational institutions, in proportion to their numbers in the population. There are also special programs, such as health care, legal assistance, allotment of land, scholarships, loans, and grants. Members of these groups are also legally protected against discrimination, such as debt, forced labor, and untouchability (Galanter 1983; Chatterji 1996; Sheth 1996; Beteille 1992).

Three main categories of people have been identified as eligible for preferential policies, the Scheduled Castes (SCs), the Scheduled Tribes (STs), and the **Other Backward Classes** (OBCs). Based on a list originally prepared in the 1930s, it is relatively easy to identify SCs and STs. Although no caste census has been taken in India since independence, it is estimated that about 15 percent of the people are SCs and about 7 percent STs. The OBCs are the non-untouchable lower-caste members, mostly Shudras, whose "backwardness" is based on social and economic disadvantages. However, no clear criteria have emerged to identify OBCs and there is enormous disagreement over whether to assign people this status on the basis of caste or on economic criteria. This problem is exacerbated by the fact that historically it has been difficult to separate caste and economic status, and even now caste-based prejudice and discrimination limit economic advancement to a considerable extent.

In the 1960s, the reservation system for SCs and STs started, but it was left to the individual states to determine groups that would be identified as OBCs. Many states identified OBCs, mainly on the basis of castes that were economically disadvantaged. Reservations and preferential policies for OBCs have been implemented more in the southern states, which have also had stronger non-Brahman movements. There has been considerable opposition to implementation of these policies in other parts of India. The Central Government, meanwhile, appointed a commission headed by B. P. Mandal to deal with the issue. The Mandal Commission Report was completed in 1978, and concluded that caste is the main reason for social and economic backwardness. The Commission determined that 52 percent of Indians could be classified as OBCs, in addition to SCs and STs. Reservation of seats in various state institutions for a certain period of time was recommended as a solution to the problem. However, acknowledging that it was not advisable to reserve such a high percentage of seats, the Commission recommended that 27 percent of seats be reserved for OBCs, in addition to 15 percent for SCs and 7 percent for STs.

Anticipating large-scale opposition to the recommendations, the Congress-led government did not implement them. However, in 1990 the Janata Dal government attempted partial implementation of the recommendations, leading to widespread unrest and opposition from middle- and upper-caste youth, intellectuals, and elites. The government was voted out of power, and a court order stayed implementation of the recommendations.

In the midst of debates and controversies over the preferential policies, there has been uneven and piecemeal implementation of policies. To the extent that the policies and programs have been implemented, they have had a significant impact on many sections among the lower castes and classes. Reservation of seats in elections to state and central government legislatures has led to increased representation of SCs, STs, and OBCs in elected offices. They have acquired strong local support and have become an important element in electoral politics. They have also gone on to form strong regional political parties. In this capacity they have formed governments in many states, or been part of coalition governments at the regional and national levels. Also people from these disadvantaged groups are to be found in larger numbers in government jobs and all levels of educational institutions.

However, only a relatively small proportion of the lower castes and classes have benefited from these policies. There is increasing economic and educational differentiation among the SCs, STs, and OBCs, and those with higher economic positions, educational skills, and connections are better able to make use of the opportunities. They are most visible in the highly coveted government jobs, although these jobs constitute only about 2 percent of the jobs in the country. They have fewer opportunities in private sector jobs. However, with limited job opportunities in India, government jobs are much sought after, as is access to technical educational institutions.

Even as there is increased visibility and acceptance of people from socially and economically disadvantaged groups, there is also more overt hostility and violence expressed against the lower castes and classes in many parts of India. For example, in parts of Bihar, upper-caste landowners formed a private army called the Ranvir Sena in 1994 to "protect" themselves. Although it is outlawed, the Ranvir Sena had by early 1999 carried out 20 massacres of Dalits (Damodaran and Ansari 1999). Much hostility is also expressed against reservations in government jobs and in institutes for technical education, particularly on the part of many from the traditionally higher castes who are economically disadvantaged. The controversy is especially great over the criteria used for eligibility for preferential policies for OBCs.

Many argue that the preferential policies are necessary to overcome the effects of past discrimination and oppression that kept whole groups at a disadvantage. They also note that individual achievements, merit, as well as economic position are still significantly affected by caste and other social conditions affecting whole groups. Others, however, counter that the system of reservations undermines individual merit and achievement. Several scholars, intellectuals, and government commissions appointed to look into the issue argue that there should be flexibility in the way in which policies are implemented, and that economic and educational disadvantages as well as social stigma and deprivation should be considered (Sheth 1996; Beteille 1992).

Ironically, the issue of preferential policies and reservations undercuts the official commitment to equal treatment of individuals from all social categories. The official goal is to eliminate caste inequality and differential treatment on the basis of caste. Debates surrounding these policies and their implementation, however, have elevated the significance of caste in Indian social life. It is important, though, not to overstate the practical impact of preferential policies. A disproportionate percentage of the poor are from the SCs, STs, and OBCs. The fact that many people from these groups now have access to social and economic advancement does not mean that merit is not considered when selecting them for certain programs and positions. A significant number of positions reserved for these groups go unfilled because of lack of qualified individuals. Many argue that more needs to be done to prepare people from disadvantaged segments to make use of opportunities open to them.

CASTE AND CLASS

Most of the discussion on social stratification in India has centered on caste. Class-based inequalities, related to ownership and control over property or lack thereof as well as income related to educational and skill level, are considered mainly in relation to caste. This is because class status has historically been connected to caste, and this continues to be the case to a significant extent even now. However, with increasing industrialization, urbanization, introduction of modern occupations, and the incorporation of India into the global economy, there has been a gradual disengagement of economic and occupational positions from caste. However, Indians are simultaneously members of a caste, class, religion, language, or gender, much as people in North America belong to a particular race, ethnicity, class, and gender. Depending on the situation, a person or group of persons may act in terms of one or more of these at one time, and another in a different context. For example, caste identity may be important in arranging a marriage or in making electoral alliances, but class interest may come into play in work-related settings.

In rural India, relationship to the land continues to be a significant factor in class relations. Broadly speaking, at the top of the hierarchy are the big landowners. Included in this category are owners of land who receive rent on their property as well as owners who hire workers to till the land. Next in rank are the middle peasants who own enough land to be able to work on, using their own and family labor and occasional hired workers, or who have tenancy rights over enough land to make a comfortable living after paying rent on the land. At the bottom are poor peasants who may own very little land or no land. Some may be poor tenants, others may work other people's land or do some additional work to add to their income, or may be sharecroppers or landless agricultural laborers. There is enormous regional variation as to the percentage of people in the different categories, statistics are incomplete and often inaccurate, and different interpretations of what constitutes a large-, medium-, or small-size landholding (Thorner 1973; Dhanagare 1991 [1983]).

Among the rural residents engaged in agricultural occupations, the big landlords and rich peasants tend to be from the upper castes, whereas the middle peasants tend to be from the middle castes. The poor peasants and tenants are still more likely to be from the lower and artisan castes, and most of the landless agricultural laborers are Dalits. For example, although 52 percent of non-Dalits own some land, only 29 percent of Dalits do so. And 55 percent of Dalits are landless agricultural laborers compared to 25 percent of the non-Dalits. And because of the seasonal and casual nature of much agricultural labor, about 60 percent of agricultural laborers are poor, resulting in a higher concentration of poverty among the Dalits (Thorat 1998).

However, with increasing commercialization and introduction of technology and capital in agriculture, it has become easier to buy and sell land. For the most part, however, the middle and rich peasants have been in a better position to acquire more land. Government land reform legislation did eliminate the largest absentee landlords, but many of the larger landowners have also been able to circumvent legislation limiting the size of holdings. Some middle and poor peasants have acquired land as a result of government legislation, and landless agricultural workers have also mobilized in several places for better wages and working conditions. However, many people have also been displaced from the land because of increases in technological inputs and population growth.

A corresponding trend has been for individuals from all agricultural classes to engage in commercial trade and entrepreneurial activities in the villages, such as retailing, machine repairs, and a variety of services and businesses. Many have moved to urban areas. Some have improved their economic position while others have experienced a decline in social status. There continues to be large-scale unemployment and underemployment. These trends reflect some disengagement between caste and class, and some movement from a "closed" system of stratification to an "open" system. However, the historical association of economic position with caste continues to influence the nature of **social mobility** for those associated with the agricultural economy.

There is more class differentiation in urban areas, as well as occupational diversity. There are large and small industrialists, entrepreneurs, middle-class professionals and bureaucrats, working classes working in a range of occupations, and the poor with uncertain, intermittent, or no employment.

Because of the range and diversity of the Indian economy (see Chapter 5) and social and occupational relations, it is difficult to classify people in India as a whole on the basis of social class. Accurate statistics are also hard to come by. According to one estimate, approximately 1 percent of Indians fall in the upper class composed of industrialists, top executives, and large property owners. Between 20 and 30 percent are in the upper-middle or middle class, a growing and consumption-oriented category, comprised of prosperous farmers, white-collar workers, small business owners, and professionals, mostly from the upper three castes. About one-third of the population is estimated to be working class, composed of small peasants, artisans, clerical workers, and industrial workers. They tend to be from many different classes. Approximately 40 percent of the population is poor, comprising those who work full time or intermittantly in rural and urban areas in manual occupations, or those who are unemployed. These categories are disproportionately OBCs and Dalits (Heitzman and Worden 1996:278–79). But there is a lot of variation in each category, and little consensus on what level of income and style of life would constitute a particular class categorization.

The big industrialists, rich farmers, and white-collar professionals in industrial and government bureaucracies are the most powerful groups in India (Bardhan 1984, 1988). A disproportionate percentage of them are from the less than 15 percent of those who constitute the upper

Social class differences in India are evident from contrasts in housing. On the left is an apartment building for urban upper-class residents, while the photo on the right shows a street in a working-class residential neighborhood.

three castes in India. In 1985, for example, nearly 38 percent of the officers in the highly influential Indian Administrative Service were Brahmans, whereas the top three castes accounted for about 70 percent of all officers. Shudras, who constitute most of the OBCs, and according to the Mandal Commission Report constitute 52 percent of the Indian population, accounted for about 2 percent of the IAS officers, whereas the rest were unidentified in terms of caste (Goyal 1989). A study of upper-level business executives of 1,100 large private corporations and state-owned companies revealed that Brahmans accounted for 43.5 percent of the executives, and the upper and middle castes constituted about 90 percent of executives (Goyal 1990). Therefore, the upper classes in India are overwhelmingly from the upper-caste groups.

The extent of inequality is difficult to measure in India. And although income is not the only measure of the quality of life, the World Bank has attempted to measure the distribution of income or consumption for all countries in the world on a standardized scale. According to the World Development Report 1997, in 1992 the richest 10 percent of Indians accounted for 28.4 percent of the share of income or consumption, and the poorest 10 percent accounted for a 3.7 percent share. The highest 20 percent accounted for a 42.6 percent share of income or consumption, and the bottom 20 percent accounted for 8.5 percent of income or consumption. Table 4–1 compares the distribution of income or consumption for India to some other countries in the world.

TABLE 4 – 1

Percentage Distribution of Income or Consumption: Selected Countries

Country	Lowest 10%	Lowest 20%	Second Quintile	Third Quintile	Fourth Quintile	Highest 20%	Highest 10%
India	3.7	8.5	12.1	15.8	21.1	42.6	28.4
United States	—	4.7	11.0	17.4	25.0	41.9	25.0
Sweden	—	8.0	13.2	17.4	24.5	36.9	20.8
Mexico	1.6	4.1	7.8	12.5	20.2	55.3	39.2
Brazil	0.7	2.1	4.9	8.9	16.8	67.5	51.3
China	2.2	5.5	9.8	14.9	22.3	47.5	30.9
Japan	—	8.7	13.2	17.5	23.1	37.5	22.4
Russia	1.2	3.7	8.5	13.5	20.4	53.8	38.7
Ghana	3.4	7.9	12.0	16.1	21.8	42.2	27.3
South Africa	1.4	3.3	5.8	9.8	17.7	63.3	47.3

Source: World Development Report, 1997.

CONCLUSION

It is clear that India is a highly differentiated and stratified society. It is also a dynamic and changing society, particularly since independence. We see that caste continues to be an important dimension of stratification and inequality in India. However, caste itself is a dynamic institution that is very diverse. Caste-based practices vary from one part of the country to another, from one sub-caste to another, from one family to another, and from one religion to another.

Overall, caste has become an important part of interest-group politics, and remains important in family rituals and in the arrangement of marital alliances. The relationship between caste and hereditary occupation is less significant now, and there are also fewer restrictions on social interaction among the castes, especially in urban areas. There are also numerous movements challenging the injustices associated with the caste system. The advent of modern economic and political trends and the influence of Western cultural patterns have also brought about a certain amount of disengagement between caste and class. It is possible to look at inequality in India in terms of economic position. However, it is still not possible to fully understand the system of stratification without looking at how caste status affects the quality of life and social mobility in modern India.

CHAPTER 5

The Economy

In the fall of 1998, coinciding with the festival season, many parts of India experienced a widespread shortage of onions, accompanied by skyrocketing prices for this key ingredient that adds a distinct flavor to many Indian dishes. As people used creative means to acquire the elusive onions, stood in lines in anticipation of getting some, and organized protests, the government scrambled to deal with the crisis by importing onions. The onion fiasco became for many a symbol of the inability of the Indian government to manage the economy effectively, leading to electoral losses for the ruling party in several state and local elections. And when the government announced an increase in prices of several essential food items sold at subsidized rates to the poor and working classes through the public distribution system in January 1999, widespread protests led to the rolling back of the price hikes. These two incidents are symptomatic of the endless battles against rising prices that Indians have been fighting since the 1960s, within a context in which most people spend a disproportionate amount of their earnings on food.

At the same time, there has been considerable industrial, technological, and commercial expansion in India in recent decades. An increasing number of Indians have acquired modern amenities and consumer goods such as TVs, VCRs, telephones, refrigerators, washing machines, food processors, scooters, and cars. This process has accelerated with the market-oriented economic reforms and liberalization since the early 1990s. However, many of these items are out of reach of most Indians, and a slowdown in sales combined with overproduction and competition, has led to a glut in the market forcing manufacturers to slash prices.

These instances highlight the fragility as well as the diversity of the Indian economy. Most people live in rural areas and are engaged in the agricultural sector of the economy. This translates into much lower income and productivity per capita when compared to the more industrialized countries. Moreover, income and wealth distribution is highly unequal, and poverty, although lower than in the 1960s, continues to be widespread. India's economy since independence is also closely tied to government policies and changes in those policies, as well as the increasing trend toward **globalization** of the economy.

In this chapter I will attempt to make sense of India's economy by first placing it within the global economic context. I will then provide a snapshot of India's economic structure in the mid-1990s and some trends since independence. This will lead into a discussion of government policies, their impact on the economy and poverty, recent economic reforms, and debates surrounding reforms and efforts to improve economic conditions.

INDIA IN THE GLOBAL ECONOMY

As is evident from the historical overview, India has had a highly complex economic system including trade and commerce with other parts of the world for many centuries. It is with the expansion of trade with Europe, however, that India became incorporated into the capitalist world system over the last 500 years. As Britain expanded its colonial rule over India, it used India as the source of raw materials, goods and resources that were necessary for industrial development in Britain. British manufactured products were then imported into India resulting in limited industrial development in India. At the time of independence, therefore, India entered the world system of states as industrially and technologically less developed when compared to the more developed countries of Western Europe and North America.

Following the **world system theory** (Wallerstein 1974), one way to assess India's place in the global economic context is to broadly categorize the countries of the world into core, peripheral, and semiperipheral economies. The **core economies** are characterized by a high level of industrialization and mechanization, occupational diversification, and stable governments. Examples of core economies are the United States, Canada, Germany, Britain, and Japan. **Peripheral economies,** on the other hand, are characterized by a low level of industrial and technological development, with an economy highly dependent on a single commodity such as tobacco, coffee, sugar, or minerals that are primarily exported as raw materials to the core countries. These commodities also typically generate a lower income than the manufactured goods mainly produced in the core countries and are susceptible to price fluctuations. Many of the poorest countries in Sub-Saharan Africa, for example, are considered peripheral economies. **Semiperipheral economies** fall in between the core and peripheral economies. Many countries, including

India, Mexico, Brazil, and several Asian and Middle Eastern countries are considered semiperipheral. They provide a significant amount of raw materials to the core but are also stable and diversified enough to be potential markets and sources of cheap labor and investment by corporations based in the core countries.

Although this threefold categorization is too broad, and there is some debate over criteria of placement into these categories, it helps us understand where India stands in the world economic system. There is also a lack of accurate statistics as well as disagreements over how best to measure various aspects of India's social and economic life. But this categorization also helps us understand why the Government of India developed policies after independence to get India out of its less developed and dependent status in the world. Before discussing those policies, however, let us take a look at India's economy as it has emerged 50 years after independence.

STRUCTURE OF INDIA'S ECONOMY

In 1995, the **primary sector** of the economy including agriculture, forestry, mining, quarrying, and fishing, accounted for 29 percent of India's gross domestic product (GDP), or the total value of goods and services produced in the country (World Bank 1997). However, approximately 64 percent of the labor force is employed in this sector. The **secondary sector** of the economy, which includes manufacturing, construction, and power generation, also accounts for 29 percent of the GDP, but employs only about 16 percent of the workforce. The **tertiary sector** of the economy, which includes provision of goods and services such as trade, transportation, finance, communications, administration, and defense, contributes 41 percent of the GDP but employs only about 20 percent of the labor force. Overall, there has been a decline in the share of the GDP in the primary sector of the economy since independence and an increase in the share of the GDP in both services and manufacturing. However, most people continue to be employed in the primary sector, while there has been a significant increase in employment in services, and only a marginal increase in employment share in the secondary sector (Rogers 1996).

The structure of the Indian economy contrasts significantly with that of the United States and other more technologically and industrially developed societies. In the United States, for example, about 72 percent of the GDP is in the tertiary sector accounting for about 69 percent of the labor force. The secondary sector accounts for 26 percent of the GDP and 28 percent of the labor force, and the primary sector accounts for only 2 percent of the GDP and 3 percent of the labor force. India is somewhat closer to China in the structure of its economy, where agriculture accounts for 21 percent of the GDP and 74 percent of the labor force, industry comprises 48 percent of the GDP and 15 percent of the labor force, and the service sector accounts for 31 percent of the GDP and 11 percent of the labor force (World Bank 1997).

Moreover, in India the conditions under which people are employed varies enormously within each sector. People may be employed either in the "organized" or the **formal sector** or the "unorganized" or the **informal sector.** The formal sector includes "modern" large-scale manufacturing, large financial and commercial services, and state-owned or public-sector undertakings such as administrative services, railroads, air transportation, telecommunications, heavy industry, and mining. This sector is characterized by secure employment, higher wages, and benefits. But by the early 1990s, only 8 percent of the Indian workforce was employed in the organized sector. An overwhelming 92 percent of the workforce, including 90 percent of the men and 96 percent of the women, are employed in the informal sector that includes most of agriculture and related occupations and numerous small enterprises employing less than 10 people, such as in fishing, handicrafts, vending, and small-scale mechanized operations. It is in the informal sector that an estimated 55 million children are employed, mostly in agriculture or services such as in retail shops, servants in homes, and in hotels. In addition, many children work with their parents in a variety of home-based enterprises such as handicrafts. Often, within the same large enterprise,

Most Indians work in what is termed the informal sector. The picture on the left shows two girls, about 10 years old, working in a brick kiln. At right, vegetable vendors sell produce at a market. Photo at left by Sharmila Joshi *(Courtesy: Women's Feature Service).*

workers may be split between those in the formal and the informal sectors. Although some in the unorganized sector may do quite well economically, for the most part this sector is characterized by poor working conditions, insecure employment, and few benefits, and protective legislation is difficult to implement. It is estimated that the informal sector contributes about 50 percent of India's GDP (Ramaswamy 1995:98–102).

Since the mid-1970s, over one million Indians have found employment in the oil-producing Middle Eastern countries and their remittances have become a key source of income and foreign exchange. India has also produced a large pool of highly skilled scientists, engineers, physicians, computer software programmers and other professionals. They, along with small entrepreneurs, white-collar workers, and farmers with sizable landholdings are part of a middle class that is estimated to be somewhere between 150 and 300 million people, depending on how they are counted (Rogers 1996:301, 325–26).

Most of the agricultural land in India is family owned or operated, and approximately 50 percent of the holdings are less than 1 hectare in size. Only about 4 percent of the farms are over 10 hectares, with the rest falling somewhere in-between. The Government of India enacted legislation to limit the size of holdings, redistribute the land among the landless, and protect small farmers and tenants. Implementation of the various legislations, however, has varied from state to state, and many have exploited loopholes in the laws to sidestep them. Moreover, a large number of holdings are unviable because of small size and lack of inputs and resources, such as seeds, fertilizers, access to credit, and technology. Although there has been an increase in capital investments, use of technology, extension services, and irrigation, there is large-scale unemployment and underemployment in rural areas, and a large proportion of workers are landless agricultural laborers or in casual and temporary employment (Bhargava 1996:386–404).

Even so, India is now self-sufficient in food production. The major crops are rice and wheat, as well as maize, millet, sorghum, beans, peas, and lentils. Among commercial cash crops, India is the largest producer of sugar in the world. Cotton is an important crop whose production has increased to meet the needs of the large cotton textile industry in India. Jute and tea are other major cash crops. Other agriculture-related activities include livestock and poultry farming, forestry, and fishing.

In manufacturing, the cotton textile industry is the single largest employer. There are a few privately owned highly mechanized textile mills, and hundreds of thousands small power-loom and handloom units in urban and rural areas. Steel, aluminum, fertilizers, and petrochemicals are other key industries, and there are both large state-owned units as well as small and large privately-owned enterprises. Since 1980, there has also been an increase in electronics, computers, and motor vehicles. Other industry-related areas include construction, energy, mining, transportation, telecommunications, and scientific and technological research.

ECONOMIC PERFORMANCE

India's economic performance since independence reflects mixed trends. There has been considerable growth and improvement in the economy. But the growth has not been as fast as many within and outside the country expected or desired. Moreover, some sections of the population, and some regions, have benefited more than others. There is intense debate on the reasons for these trends and also criticism of an exclusive focus on growth of GDP as an indicator of economic performance. Some of these issues will be incorporated into the discussion that follows; however, a look at growth in terms of GDP does provide a useful starting point in attempting to comprehend the Indian economy.

Between 1950 and 1980, India's GDP rose at an average annual rate of 3.58 percent, but the rate accelerated to an average annual growth rate of 5.8 percent between 1980 and 1990, before slowing down to 4.6 percent between 1990 and 1995. Per capita income, meanwhile, doubled between 1950 and 1990, but about half that growth came after 1980 when the GDP grew faster and the rate of population growth slowed (Dandekar 1994:8–9; World Bank 1997). According to Government of India estimates, the GDP grew at the rate of 7.5 percent in 1996–97, but slowed to post a growth of 5 percent in 1997–98. It is expected to grow at the rate of 5.8 percent in 1998–99 (*Times of India*, February 10, 1999).

Growth in the agricultural sector has been slower than in the industrial sector. Agricultural production grew at a rate of 2.45 percent per year between 1950 and 1990 and India became self-sufficient in meeting its needs. But the growth rate was 3.37 percent per year during the 1980s. The industrial sector, meanwhile, grew at a rate of 5.33 percent per year between 1950 and 1980, posting a growth rate of 7.25 percent per year during the 1980s (Dandekar 1994:13–16).

On average, India's GDP has grown faster than many North American and European countries between 1985 and 1995, but slower than most East Asian countries such as Taiwan, China, South Korea, and Thailand. However, East and Southeast Asian economies have faced a sharp recession since 1997, and India and China are the only major Asian economies expected to post a growth in 1998–99.

Within India, between 1960 and 1970 those states that were at the lower end in terms of GDP remained there whereas those at the top stayed at the top. Moreover, the gap between the highest and lowest states in terms of GDP increased. For example, the states of Bihar, Madhya Pradesh, Uttar Pradesh, and Orissa stayed at the bottom, and Punjab,

Gujarat, and Maharashtra stayed at the top. Only West Bengal experienced a drop from the second to the ninth place nationally, and Haryana
rose from the tenth to the second place (Dandekar 1994:10). The regions
experiencing lower levels of industrial and agricultural development also
exhibit higher levels of poverty and deprivation.

Although there is considerable fluctuation in prices, the rate of inflation based on the wholesale price index has been controlled in the
1990s, and has remained under 10 percent for nearly four years, and in
January 1999 stood at 4.44 percent. Ordinary Indian citizens, however,
complain that the prices they pay for food and other essential commodities increase at a much faster pace, and dispute official figures. Indeed,
the inflation rate based on the consumer price index stood at 15.32 percent in January 1999, although it was lower than the previous month's
figure of 19.67 percent (*Times of India,* February 1, 1999). The hardest hit
are the people working in the informal sector of the economy because
their wages and salaries are not linked to inflation.

These economic trends can be better understood by looking at the
policies of the Indian government since independence, the consequences
of those policies and the debates about them, as well as recent reforms.

ECONOMIC POLICIES AND PROCESSES

The Government of India has been a major player in managing and regu-
lating the Indian economy. The main aim soon after independence was
to promote economic growth and modernization by improving industrial and agricultural production, eradicating poverty, and achieving
self-reliance. A related goal was to promote economic equality and social
justice on the basis of democratic principles of protecting individual freedoms, fundamental rights, and electoral politics. In order to develop and
execute these often contradictory aims, the Indian government launched
a program of "planned economic development" in 1950, with successive
"five-year plans" to guide the economy. In the early years after independence there was a fair degree of consensus that state-orchestrated
planned development was the best way to develop Indian economy and
society. Although private enterprise and ownership of property was to
be allowed, the nature of private enterprise, industry, and agriculture
was to be closely watched and regulated by the state (Frankel
1978:71–112; Bagchi 1995; Chaudhuri 1995). Indian economy is, therefore,
often described as a "mixed economy": a mixture between **capitalism,** in
which resources and means of producing goods and services are privately owned, and **socialism,** in which resources and means of production are collectively owned and usually controlled by the state. In order
to move toward the planned goals, the Indian government is working simultaneously on the agricultural and industrial sectors, and is developing the infrastructure to support economic development.

In the sphere of agriculture, the government first set out to bring about a more egalitarian system of land ownership and control as a prelude to an increase in efficiency and production. As a result, most of the biggest absentee landlords were eliminated and ownership of some of the land passed on to the actual tillers. However, legislations limiting the size of landholdings and improving the position of tenants and small landowners were only partially implemented or sidestepped. The distribution of ownership and control of agricultural land, therefore, continued to remain unequal. In order to exhibit some adherence to Gandhi's philosophy of voluntary participation and local self-government, the government professed to mobilize the rural masses to promote justice and equity in social and economic relations. Realizing, however, that the process of change at this level would be a slow one, the government focused on industrialization as the vehicle for rapid economic growth.

The industrial strategy was to promote both state-owned **public sector enterprises** and private industry but under close state supervision. The government, therefore, assumed the task of the development of heavy industry and infrastructure in the areas such as mining, iron and steel, machinery and tools, power generation, air and rail transportation, energy, and telecommunications. This entailed heavy capital investment with returns accruing only in the long term, and led to the growth of the public sector. To promote savings and self-reliance, the government instituted a policy of "import substitution" under which the import of consumer goods was severely limited. The plan was to initially keep the demand for consumer goods low and meet these needs through small-scale and village-based industries and production of handicrafts. Private enterprise was to be closely regulated, a license was required to start any new enterprise, and there were limits on the size of enterprises and the types of products they could produce. Numerous tariffs and duties limited trade and commerce. Limited foreign investment was allowed, and **multinational corporations** were required to keep 51 percent of the equity share within India (Rubin 1986).

Consensus on these policies of planned development, however, started to break down in the mid-1960s as contradictions began to emerge. Changes in the agricultural sector were very slow. There was little redistribution of land, and institutions of local self-government did not develop sufficiently to alter inegalitarian social relations. There was increasing pressure for investment in high-tech agricultural practices, such as mechanization, use of fertilizers and pesticides, and high-yielding varieties of crops in order to boost production. Much of this investment took place in areas that were already well placed in terms of infrastructures such as irrigation and among middle- and upper-level peasant proprietors with relatively large-sized holdings, and promoted more egalitarian social relations. The areas that experienced most investment were Punjab, Haryana, western Uttar Pradesh, and parts of many other states such as Maharashtra, Madras (now Tamil Nadu), Karnataka, and Gujarat. Investment was slowest in the central and eastern parts of India. Later, after the 1970s, investment also picked up in many other regions while slowing in some. For the most part, however, the middle and upper peasantry, usually in the middle and upper castes, were in the best position to take advantage of opportunities such as loans to invest in agricultural inputs. Many small farmers and tenants have been displaced from their lands, and agricultural wage laborers have lost employment opportunities. This process has increased concentration of economic resources in fewer hands and exacerbated poverty and deprivation. At the same time, however, agricultural production increased rapidly during the 1970s and by the end of the decade India became self-sufficient in food production (Frankel 1978:113–55; Srivastava 1995).

Initially there was an expectation that rapid industrialization would provide more opportunities for employment. There was growth in industrial investment until the mid-1960s mainly because of the expansion of the public sector. Industrial growth slowed thereafter because of lower investment in the public sector and inefficiencies relating to state regulation of industry. The expansion of the public sector has created a huge bureaucracy and the returns on investment in heavy industry and infrastructure are limited. Many public sector enterprises have run up huge losses, but the government has continued to subsidize them because they are one of the few sources of stable employment in the economy. Government regulations and licensing procedures have led to increased bureaucracy, inordinate delays, controls, and corruption. Protection of Indian private enterprise from foreign and domestic competition, has also limited motivation to improve the quality of products and technological development (Frankel 1978; Dandekar 1994:16–18; Sathyamurthy 1995).

After the economic slowdown and crisis in the late 1960s, the government has been compelled to gradually relax controls on foreign capital, increase subsidies to the public sector, and also the private sector enterprises to keep them from collapsing, and borrow money to meet needs. In the private sector the government increased opportunities for investment in small-scale industries, leading to the creation of a new and larger skilled business and industrial class. These groups, as well as the newly emerging skilled workers and professionals, started demanding further liberalization of bureaucratic controls on the economy in the last two decades. However, as in the agricultural sector, industrial growth has taken place in an uneven manner. A significant amount of the growth has taken place around the major port cities of Bombay, Calcutta, and Madras (now Chennai). But there also has been growth around Delhi, Haryana, Punjab, and Karnataka. Small-scale industry has developed around smaller towns in several states. Public sector investment has taken place largely in areas that are rich in natural resources, such as parts of Bihar, Orissa, and Madhya Pradesh and the North-East (Baru 1995).

Overall, the trend toward capitalist economic development has led to the creation of a sizable entrepreneurial and professional middle class and upper class. Agricultural and industrial growth, although slow, are still much higher than under British rule. Indian industry has diversified, and India has achieved a considerable amount of self-reliance. On the other hand, however, there has also been large-scale unemployment and underemployment in rural and urban areas. As for the five-year plans, they continue to be formulated, but for decades now implementation has been problematic, and targets have not been met. Associated with uneven capitalist economic development is the continuation of widespread poverty.

POVERTY IN INDIA

The continuation of poverty is one of the biggest failures of economic policy and development in India since independence. There is considerable disagreement over how to measure poverty, and also over the extent of poverty. There is also debate on the reasons for poverty, and measures to deal with poverty. Furthermore, poverty everywhere is associated with social inequalities, which in the case of India are fundamentally tied to caste, gender, and tribal status.

According to recent estimates, approximately 40 percent of India's population live in poverty, accounting for about 385 million people (Gupta 1996:151). In comparison, the poverty rate in the United States is about 13 percent, and ranges from 3 to 6 percent in most Western European countries. The poverty rate in India is lower only than several countries in Sub-Saharan Africa. The poverty line as defined by the Government of India in 1992 was placed at an income and consumption level equivalent to Rs 255.20 (the equivalent of about $10 at that time) per capita per month in urban areas, and Rs 187.05 ($7.50) per capita per month in rural areas. The poverty line in India is based on the expense necessary to provide the required number of calories of food per person per day. Other basic needs for human existence, therefore, are not included in arriving at the poverty line. The World Bank defines the poverty level at the equivalent of $1 U.S. per person per day. By that measure, in 1995 about 52.5 percent of people in India were below the poverty line, and the U.S. dollar was valued at about Rs 35 (World Bank 1997). It is important to keep in mind, however, that the equivalent of a U.S. dollar buys different quantities of goods in different countries, and what may be perceived as basic needs in the United States are not necessarily considered essential in India. It is true, however, that with the introduction of foreign consumer goods and media sources, there has been a significant change in consumption patterns and desires that go largely unmet. Another complicating factor is that many people, particularly in rural areas, may meet many of their needs through exchange and sharing of goods and services, and these transactions may not be counted or reported. By the same token, however, the actual extent of deprivation and poverty may also be underreported.

Government of India figures show that at 40.7 percent in 1992, the level of poverty in India was significantly below the 1971 level of 55.1 percent. In terms of absolute numbers, however, the actual number of people below the poverty line increased during that time from 301.8 to 354.8 million because of population growth. The official poverty rate had declined to about 35 percent in the late 1980s before rising above 40 percent in the early 1990s (Gupta 1996:151). However, there is some variation from year to year and recent World Bank estimates indicate a gradual decline in poverty. Some argue that a higher GDP and growth rate is the key to reducing poverty; others argue that government-backed poverty alleviation programs and mobilization of the poor to fight for their rights are the key. A combination of all these factors are probably responsible. However, in other East Asian countries, such as China, Thailand, South Korea, and Indonesia, poverty has declined much more rapidly than in India, from about 35 percent in 1970 to 10 percent in 1990 overall (Gupta 1996:168). These countries have also experienced faster economic growth than India during this time, as well as improvements in social conditions such as education and health care.

Within India, the rate of poverty is higher in rural areas than in urban areas, averaging about 45 percent in the former and 36.5 percent in the latter in 1987–88 (Dreze and Sen 1995:216). And higher poverty levels exist in the eastern and central sections, mainly in Bihar, West Bengal, Eastern Uttar Pradesh, Orissa, Madhya Pradesh, and parts of Gujarat, Maharashtra, Rajasthan, Andhra Pradesh, and Tamil Nadu, exceeding 60 percent in many sections. On the other hand, poverty is below 5 percent in the states of Punjab and Haryana and parts of Jammu and Kashmir (Heston 1990, 106–111).

The Government of India has undertaken numerous economic and social measures in rural and urban areas to alleviate poverty. They have met with modest success (Vaidyanathan 1995; Nayyar 1996). In the rural areas, the government instituted social and political reforms alongside economic development programs. Land reform legislation to redistribute ownership and control of land more equitably, revival of institutions of local self-government, and electoral democracy were expected to enable small farmers, peasants, lower castes, landless agricultural workers, and other underprivileged groups to benefit from economic development programs. Programs introduced over the last few decades include improvements in infrastructure to create employment opportunities for the landless and marginal farmers; improved access to credit, inputs, and extension services for smaller farmers to increase yields; employment generation and training programs targeted at youth; a variety of programs for women and children; health and education programs.

For the most part, however, funds for these programs have remained under the control of central and state government bureaucrats. In the local areas, mostly those with connections to local bureaucrats and politicians, usually from the upper- and middle-status groups, were in a position to make use of the opportunities. Among the lower castes and tribes, however, mostly those who were better off were able to participate in economic development programs. Until recently, women were for the most part excluded from economic empowerment programs, even though they officially account for about 32 percent of the labor force. They were mainly included in health and social welfare programs. Many of the people who were supposed to be beneficiaries of the programs were often unaware of the programs or their eligibility for them. In many instances, various intermediaries responsible for implementing the programs have used the resources for the benefit of their own families and relatives.

In urban areas, poverty alleviation programs have focused mainly on providing food and essential commodities at a subsidized rate, health services, housing, civic amenities, education, and employment. But, as in the rural areas, implementation has been partially successful even as large numbers of people displaced from rural areas migrate to the cities that lack the infrastructure to accommodate the migrants (Kundu 1996).

However, since the late 1960s there has been a lot of mobilization among the poor and illiterate to demand a fairer share of resources. As discussed in the chapters on stratification, gender relations, and politics in India, there has been an enormous increase in grassroots activism and social movements among the poor, women, Dalits, peasants, and tribal groups on a variety of issues. Numerous non-government voluntary organizations have also become active in working with these groups. There is considerable evidence that where the local poor and disadvantaged are organized, voluntary agencies are active, and there is more decentralized control over the programs, poverty alleviation programs are more successful in reaching the groups they are designed for. This is particularly the case when programs for income generation are connected to health, literacy, and education for women, children, the Dalits, and tribal populations. These trends underscore the point that poverty is not just an issue of lack of money or material resources, but is an inextricable part of unequal social relations tied to gender, caste, and tribe.

RECENT ECONOMIC REFORMS AND LIBERALIZATION

Ever since the economic crisis of the late 1960s, the Indian government has been under increasing pressure to undertake **economic reforms** in the direction of more freedom for private enterprise and commercialization, and less government regulation. The pressure for reforms has come from the newly emerging powerful groups such as middle and rich peasants, small-scale entrepreneurs and industrialists, and urban middle classes and professionals. In addition, international agencies such as the World Bank, the International Monetary Fund, and the more industrialized countries in the core sector have pressured India to open up its economy to foreign capital, to reduce internal controls, and to institute free market reforms. These reforms have also been a condition attached to money borrowed to deal with economic crises, deficits, and inflation in the last two decades.

Some liberalization, technological innovations, and commercialization have taken place since the late 1970s, accelerating even more during the 1980s. However, it was after its return to power in 1991 that the Congress-led government announced the most comprehensive program for economic reforms and liberalization. Political instability and uncertainty associated with India's third general elections since 1996, have stalled reforms somewhat. As the reforms have been partially implemented, and continuously reformulated and modified, there has been a wide-ranging debate on the merits of the policy, the actual nature of the reforms, and the unfolding consequences of the reforms.

Main reform proposals are concerned with reducing government control of private sector industrial projects; eliminating government licenses for setting up new projects; expanding production without obtaining prior government permission; reducing or eliminating import

Information technology professionals at a computer software and data processing company. Such enterprises have grown at a rapid pace in India, and most of the business is contracted from overseas, highlighting the process of globalization.

duties and tariffs; expanding investments by foreign multinational companies in both infrastructures, such as power generation, oil exploration,
telecommunications, as well as consumer goods; permitting foreign companies to own more than 51 percent of the equity; reducing subsidies to
farmers; reorganizing the public sector enterprises by making them more
efficient, privatizing some, closing some, and reducing others in size.

There has, indeed, been more liberalization and the loosening of
some government controls. But benefits from the reforms have been unevenly distributed. Those who support rapid implementation of the reforms include many economists and intellectuals, the new business
classes, urban professionals, and bureaucrats. They argue that the negative outcomes are due to the slow pace of implementation and the variety of interest groups that want to protect their positions (Desai 1995).

Significant opposition to reforms is coming from those in organized
labor in the public sector undertakings who want to protect their jobs. So
far the reductions in these enterprises have come mainly from early re-
tirements and voluntary resignation rather than from laying off workers.
Some sectors of the large private industrial houses in India are opposing
rapid foreign investment. Many conservative political parties, such as the
BJP that came to power in India earlier in 1998, state that reforms are
necessary, but that foreign investment must be limited to arenas that are
deemed to be in the national interest. However, their interpretation of
national interest differs from others. There is also opposition from many
groups to the General Agreement on Tariffs and Trade or GATT that is
deemed to be beneficial to foreign multinational companies. Key proposals under GATT would force India to eliminate import duties on foreign
goods, and limit production in India of goods such as seeds, pharmaceu-
ticals, and herbal products for which foreign companies own or claim
patents, but which many Indians claim are indigenous forms of shared
knowledge (Ramaswamy 1995:115–28).

Several activists, intellectuals, and others associated with **non-
government organizations** believe that the reforms are being dictated by
international aid agencies and foreign capital that serve foreign interests
and undermine Indian sovereignty and self-reliance. They argue that this
will make India more dependent on the vagaries of global capitalism,
and serve the interests of the Indian rich and middle classes to the detri-
ment of the poor, smaller peasants, and entrepreneurs. They present
some evidence to show that economic liberalization has led to reductions
in social spending on health, education, and welfare. And the growth in
infrastructure has not been fast enough to generate employment for the
rural and urban poor resulting in slow growth in employment and
wages, and the continuation of poverty (Kumar 1991; Gupta 1996; Nayyar 1996).

Some argue that instead of opening up to foreign capital too
rapidly or worrying too much about foreign interests, the focus should

be on reforming the Indian economic and social structure from within. This would entail more efficiency and competition in the private sector in India to produce better-quality goods for the Indian market, and getting rid of the control of Indian bureaucrats and industrialists who exploit the poor, engage in bribery and corruption, and restrict small-scale farming, entrepreneurship, and trade. Alongside, efforts should be made to increase opportunities for education, employment, health care, and improving the quality of life by promoting egalitarian social and economic relations (Bagchi 1991; Kappen 1994; Kishwar 1996a).

Dreze and Sen (1995), for example, cite extensive evidence to assert that the focus on growth and free market reforms alone does not guarantee improvement in the quality of life unless accompanied by a more equitable distribution of resources and opportunities. They note that the rapid growth in many East Asian countries until the recent economic slowdown in Hong Kong, Taiwan, China, Thailand, and South Korea, for instance, occurred alongside or was consequent upon concerted efforts by the government to expand education and health care, reform of the agricultural sector, and management of the economy. In Brazil, meanwhile, rapid growth has not improved the quality of life of a large segment of the population.

It is clear that India has been unable to lift millions out of poverty, or provide adequate education, health care, and employment to millions, or deal consistently with caste and gender inequalities. In fact, India (as part of South Asia) is above only Sub-Saharan Africa in terms of the Human Development Index (HDI) constructed by the United Nations Development Program on the basis of GDP per capita, literacy rate, and the level of education, and life expectancy at birth. With 1.0 being the highest, the HDI was .44 for South Asia in 1997 and .35 for Sub-Saharan Africa. All other regions of the world have a higher HDI than South Asia, with Anglo-America being the highest at .95, followed by Japan (.94), Western Europe (.93), Latin America (.80), Eastern Europe (.78), Southeast Asia (.67), and the Middle East (.66) (Rubenstein 1999:305–14). Although there are many variations within each region and within India, and there are deficiencies in measurement techniques, the HDI does provide a rough estimate of the situation in South Asia in relation to other parts of the world.

CONCLUSION

We have seen that India's economy is vast and diverse. Since independence there have been many changes. It has grown considerably, but not as fast as many would have liked. Overall, the reforms are continuing but at a slow pace and with mixed results. Some segments are gaining, whereas others are losing. Growth continues at a moderate pace and inflation has been controlled somewhat. Many believe that a slower pace of change is better in the long run, and opening up to the global economic forces should be limited. There is some merit to the argument that the initial focus on self-reliance and indigenous economic development has created many strong sectors in the economy. There has been an expansion of the modern entrepreneurial and middle class, as well as professionals. Some argue that because of a large and complex indigenous economy and less dependence on foreign capital, the Indian economy has remained relatively untouched by the economic crisis in other Asian countries since 1997. Many Indians also cite the fact that because only about 5 to 10 percent of India's GDP is related to foreign capital, it will not be significantly affected by sanctions imposed by some industrialized countries on foreign development aid to India after India conducted nuclear tests in May 1998.

On the other hand, however, we have also noted that the slow and uneven pace of social and economic change has left millions of people in poverty, and lacking access to basic human services such as health care, education, as well as adequate employment. The large and cumbersome bureaucracy, corruption, unstable governments, lack of resources, as well as mismanagement, all are part of the problem. Many Indians take a great deal of pride in its functioning democratic institutions; its nuclear power capabilities; its scientific, technological, and economic achievements; its cultural and religious diversity, and its long history as a civilization. But they also express frustration at its failure to eradicate poverty and invest in human social development.

CHAPTER 6

Gender Relations

When I was 16 years old I first remember conversing with my father over my future as a woman in India. He stated that my sister and I could continue our formal education until we got married, and even write the entrance examinations for the highly prestigious Indian Administrative Service. However, we could only work in a paid capacity if, once married, our respective husbands allowed it! My father was expressing what he understood to be appropriate according to Indian traditions. He was reflecting one cultural ideal in India of a woman being the responsibility of her father first, then her husband, and her son if she were widowed. Expectations placed on my brother, of course, were quite different. This conversation took place in the 1970s when Indira Gandhi had been India's prime minister for several years, being only the second woman in the world to attain that position. Needless to add, my sister and I both went on to obtain doctoral degrees and become college professors. And my father always expressed enormous pride over our achievements! At the same time, about 60 percent of women in India are illiterate according to the 1991 census. Large sections of girls and women remain in a fundamentally subordinate status compared to boys and men. They face numerous barriers to equality in education, health care, work, and family life, and endure violence and discrimination.

This reflects the diverse and contrary positions occupied by women in India. India is full of examples of strong, assertive, and powerful women, as well as widespread asymmetry in gender roles and relationships. And these roles and statuses have continually changed. One way to comprehend these diversities is to realize that all human societies have social arrangements differentiating males and females on the basis of their appropriate roles, appearance, and behaviors. These arrangements rest to some extent on biological differences between females and males, and often become the basis of **gender** inequality. In India, as elsewhere, the issue of gender is a central feature of social and cultural discourse and reality.

In this chapter I explore cultural ideals and practices relating to gender in India, followed by a discussion of the issue of women's role and status during British rule in India. The rest of the chapter focuses on a variety of issues relating to gender, particularly women, in the post-independence period. These include state policies and laws relating to gender and the family, women's work and social status, the numerous efforts to overcome women's oppression as part of the Indian women's movement, and the participation of women in formal politics.

WOMEN IN HINDU INDIAN TRADITION AND HISTORY

What strikes most Western observers of Indian society is the coexistence of contradictory images and practices concerning women and men. On the one hand, India has a **patriarchal** social structure in which males have higher status and authority and women have lower status and are expected to be passive and submissive. On the other hand, we see the worship of numerous goddesses who are very strong and symbolize the power and strength of women. More recently, India has had a strong female prime minister, and has produced many artists, scholars, writers, professionals, activists, scientists, and even an astronaut.

In the dominant Hindu ideology that developed over the course of several centuries, the female is both benevolent and fertile, as well as strong, aggressive, and even destructive. These two images of a female are based on the notion that a female represents both **sakti** or energy and power, and **prakriti** or nature. The *sakti* is the source of creativity and life, but is considered dangerous if combined with *prakriti,* which is untamed and undifferentiated matter. The dangerous forces of nature, therefore, need to be harnessed and controlled. The complementary male force represented by the **purusa,** or the cosmic person, is considered appropriate for the task (Wadley 1988:23–29). Many historians believe that in pre-Aryan India **matrilineal** family organization was widespread, and many female gods were worshipped. Brahmanic Hinduism incorporated the image of the goddess as a symbol of fertility. But it sought to control the power that derived from her fertility, mainly through controlling the sexual energy of the goddess, usually by turning her into a wife or consort of a male god. In this role, the goddesses were reconfigured as benevolent and passive (Liddle and Joshi 1989:51–52).

In classical Hindu texts, therefore, there is a lot of emphasis on female behavior and its control by males. Passages from the **Laws of Manu,** written in the early part of the Christian era, note, "In childhood a female must be subject to her father, in youth to her husband, and when her lord is dead, to her sons; a woman must never be independent" (Wadley 1988:30). Men, for their part, are asked to "strive to guard their wives" in order to check their sexual desires. The role of the good, benevolent, dutiful, and controlled wife is extolled in various myths and legends, both classical and folk. Although idealized as the mother, a woman's power as the giver of life is also seen as dangerous, for being a mother gives her control over her fertility and her children. Folk and local traditions also focus on wifely duties and behaviors. However, in these traditions women have found greater avenues for self-expression. We also find women expressing their love and desire for their husbands, and their dismay at the lack of response from husbands. They also discuss relationships with other family members (Wadley 1988:29–35).

As the caste system came to be formulated and institutionalized, control over females became a means to improve and maintain caste status. One way to do so was by controlling female sexuality through arranged marriage, child marriage, prohibition of divorce, monogamy for women, and limiting a woman's contact with her natal family. The second way was to render the woman economically powerless by disinheriting her, removing her from productive labor, and secluding her from public life. However, these restrictions were stronger among the upper castes than among the lower. The lower-caste women were an important source of agricultural and household labor, and this was associated with somewhat higher status and greater rights within their group. Also, there was a lot of variation among the castes, and from one region to another. Many upper-caste women did acquire some education. And women in the commercial castes participated in many business activities (Liddle and Joshi 1989:52–56).

Over the centuries, moreover, as noted earlier, Brahmanic Hinduism has continuously been challenged. These critiques have come from Buddhism, Jainism, Sikhism, as well as lower castes. Tantric religion in the form of fertility worship and cults of the mother goddess originated in the non-Aryan regions of the northeast. The Bhakti movement also appealed to women and lower castes by providing an avenue for freedom and self-expression (Liddle and Joshi 1989:57–69). Even in the Brahmanic epics, such as the *Ramayana* and the *Mahabharata,* some versions depict good women as passive, benevolent, and subservient; others focus on women's strengths and assertiveness in the face of challenges. The interpretation of women was often linked to the ways in which stories were told in relation to local social and economic conditions and traditions (Thapar 1987:2–14).

Historically as well as in religious ideology, therefore, we find images of strong and powerful women in India, as well as the passive and subservient. There is a coexistence and often tension between the two viewpoints, but it is not unusual for Indians to see women in roles other than that of the wife and mother. This has made it possible for women to challenge and live outside of conventions. It has also allowed many women and others to advocate social changes to raise the status of women in India, and promote gender equality.

THE BRITISH IN INDIA AND INDIAN WOMEN

When the British established their rule in India, they found many aspects of Hindu and Muslim Indian cultural practices to be appalling and strange. They were particularly critical of the caste system, especially untouchability, and the subordinate position of women. They turned their attention to several practices that affected women in particular, such as child marriage, prohibition of widow remarriage, **sati** or the burning of a widow on the funeral pyre of her dead husband, female infanticide, purdah or seclusion of women, **polygyny,** and so forth. These practices were more prevalent in some parts of the country among some castes, particularly the higher castes.

Although some Indians argued that women in fact occupied a high status in Indian society, others agreed that several practices undermined the inclusive philosophy of Hinduism, and that there was a need to restore Indian women to the higher status that they were believed to have occupied in the "golden age" of Hinduism in the past. As part of the reform movement during the 19th century, *sati* was abolished in 1829, widow remarriage was allowed under the Widow Remarriage Act of 1856, and education for women was advocated. These early reforms were mainly led by men on behalf of women and had limited effect on actual practices. And they did not fundamentally challenge the patriarchal system that subordinated women. However, mainly in urban areas and among the upper castes, many women became educated and involved in public life. Many writers and poets, such as Rassundari Devi, Muktabai, Sarojini Naidu, Rokeya Sakhawat Hossain, also emerged to write about their own lives as women and commented on social issues (Forbes 1996:10–31; Tharu and Lalita 1991).

Many women, Christian missionaries, Indian social reformers, and philanthropists opened many schools and other educational institutions for the formal education of females during the late 19th century and the first few decades of the 20th century. However, by the time of independence there were still only 30 girls for every 100 boys in schools, and even fewer in higher education. Most of the girls who got educated were from the upper and middle castes mostly in urban areas (Forbes 1996:32–63; Chanana 1996).

The nature of education for women and men differed, however, on the basis of perceived appropriate social roles for women and men. Alongside the introduction of modern enterprises, commerce, services, and professions, it became more appropriate to educate males to achieve higher-status jobs in these fields. For females, education was considered necessary for them to be effective agents for the socialization of children, and to take care of family needs and support the professional pursuits of their husbands. They were taught subjects such as home science, hygiene, music, needlework, as well as basic reading, writing, and mathematics. Women were also trained as school teachers as well as physicians, but in specialties oriented to the health care needs of women and children (Chanana 1996:113–24, 138–41).

Among some sections of the Western-oriented urban middle and upper classes in India, the home became increasingly separated from the workplace. The **cult of true womanhood** reached India by the late 19th century to idealize the role of women as full-time homemakers and mothers, whereas males were viewed as the primary breadwinners. Although it reinforced the traditional roles of males and females, the focus was on somewhat greater rights for women and humanizing the family. This was true also of some women's organizations that emerged between 1917 and 1927, such as the Indian Women's Association, the National Council of Women in India, and the All India Women's Conference.

Little attention was paid to the needs and roles of poor, lower-caste, working-class, and rural women. Also, issues of women in the paid labor force were not addressed. During the 1930s and 1940s some women's groups, such as the All India Women's Conference, turned to take on issues affecting women in the paid labor force, although they still viewed this work as supplementing the family income out of necessity. The productive labor of women within their joint family enterprises, such as agriculture-related activities and craft work in rural areas, was rendered invisible. The work of poor and lower-caste women was also ignored.

In actual practice, women's economic roles diversified in many ways under British rule, and were limited in some ways. For example, opportunities for middle-class and educated women did open up in teaching, law, and medicine. However, with increasing industrialization, centralization of production in larger factories, and commercialization of trade and agriculture, many women as well as men were displaced from agricultural and nonagricultural activities in rural areas. Women's participation, for instance, gradually declined in small-scale enterprises such as food processing, dairy, pottery, rice-husking, sewing, shoe-making, and so on. Many women found jobs in factories, mines, construction, and plantations as wage laborers, often having less control over their work and working in exploitative conditions. Women also found work as domestics, and as prostitutes in urban areas.

Ironically, as women started finding work in new fields, protective legislation dealing with work that was considered "dangerous," for women, such as work in underground mines and in many kinds of factory work, led to increasing removal of women from many occupations from the late 1920s onward. Middle-class reformers focused on issues, such as sanitation, nutrition, limiting the hours of work, providing child care, and so forth. But they did not provide alternatives for women, or even recognize that many women simply had to be in the paid labor force in order to support their families (Forbes 1996:157–88).

GENDER AND SOCIETY SINCE INDEPENDENCE

Gender relations and women's lives in India since independence have unfolded within the context of state policies and laws, particularly those relating to women and families, as well as the Indian women's movement. As already discussed, there were efforts to improve the status of women in India before independence. Many Indian women also participated in the nationalist movement for independence against Britain, and also joined radical and revolutionary groups. But Gandhi, the nationalist leader who championed the cause of women and their role in the nationalist movement, focused on women's strengths in their traditional roles as self-sacrificing and self-reliant people. These qualities were perceived as an important part of one's service to the family, the community, and the nation. Gandhi did, however, open up the possibility of women's activism in public life, and exalted women's character and actions. However, Gandhi did not fundamentally challenge the patriarchal structures that limited women's roles (Kishwar 1986).

Once India became independent, the Constitution guaranteed equal rights to women and men under the law, and guaranteed full adult franchise. However, no concerted effort was made to challenge and change patriarchal social institutions. For example, as noted in Chapter 7 on the family, the laws relating to family life were recognized as part of the religious personal laws of each religion. The state, therefore, did not consider it appropriate to interfere in what it recognized as the internal affairs of each religion. And the personal laws related to each religion govern issues such as gender roles within the family, property inheritance, marriage, divorce, maintenance, and child custody. In most instances, women are in a subordinate position with regard to the personal laws. Although equality in women's education and employment are advocated, these are seen as necessary for women to be more effective in taking care of their family needs, or in occupational roles that are an extension of women's traditional roles, such as teaching and nursing. It was also assumed that women's education would make them more responsive to the government-sponsored "family planning" programs (Mahanta 1994).

Since the mid-1980s there has been a change in the state rhetoric relating to women in response to the ongoing women's movement in India. In *The National Perspective Plan for Women: 1988–2000* (1988), for example, women are not just viewed as targets for various welfare programs, or only within the traditional family context. The need to incorporate women into the overall social, economic, and political process through access to institutions and resources is stressed. Another report, *Shramshakti: Report of the National Commission on Self-Employed Women and Women in the Informal Sector* (1988), also criticized existing programs, focused on women's productive roles, and recommended measures to improve women's lives and access to resources (Kishwar and Vanita 1989). Similarly, *The National Policy for the Empowerment of Women* presented in 1996 (Haider 1996 and 1997b) recommends a series of measures for women's economic and social empowerment. In all the reports, however, there are no specific insights into how the recommendations are to be carried out in practice. It is assumed, particularly in the last-mentioned report, that women are in a position to make use of opportunities and resources that are made available. The position of women in families and their relations with men are not addressed in an explicit manner. Women still have the responsibility for most household and childbearing tasks. Economic employment, although important and necessary, only adds to the responsibilities of women unless roles and relationships within the family change and become more egalitarian.

WOMEN'S WORK AND SOCIAL STATUS

The productive activities of members of a household that are necessary for family well-being and survival also affect the social status and prestige of each member of the family. But what is considered productive work, and the level of importance attached to it, is connected to notions of masculinity and femininity and appropriate roles for females and males. For the most part, work done "outside" the house and/or work that gets paid in some manner gets counted as work. And work done "inside" the homes, which is often unpaid work, is not conceptualized as work. Most of the work that men do is "outside" work, whereas women do most of the "inside" work. As a result, much of women's work does not get counted as work in officially collected statistics. In India, as in many other parts of the world, therefore, women make an important economic contribution, but their work is often made invisible.

Among many small farmers and landless agricultural workers, work is done as a family unit. Both women and men perform productive, but interdependent, tasks. Women do most household tasks and dairying in addition to working in the fields. However, usually it is the men who are interviewed by census takers, and they often tend to under-report the work of women, especially among small cultivators. Not allowing women to work is considered a sign of prestige. Among lower-status agricultural workers, however, it is more difficult to hide work done in the fields. Women's work is hidden more in the wheat-growing area, especially in

the north. In the rice-growing areas, however, women's work is more visible, and women constitute about half of all agricultural laborers (Epstein
1996:38–44).

In a South Indian village, Mencher (1996:56–78) found that women
in the higher castes do not work in the fields, but among the larger land-
owning households they supervise agricultural operations or cook for
workers and prepare seeds for sowing. Many women also engage in unpaid family labor in order to reduce labor costs and compensate for
higher costs for fertilizers, seeds, and newer technologies. Among the
smaller landholders, women have more control over the finances than
among the larger landholders.

In general, there is higher participation of women in the paid labor
force the further south, east, and west one goes. Higher caste and class
status is usually associated with lower participation in paid work. And
Muslim women have lower rates than non-Muslims. According to World
Bank estimates, about 33 percent of females and 63 percent of males
above age five were in the paid labor force in 1983–84. However, if activities like dairying, poultry, cultivating vegetables, and collecting fodder
and firewood are counted, it is estimated that about 51 percent of females are in the labor force (United Nations 1995:34–35). According to
the Census of India, in 1991, 51.55 percent of males and 22.25 percent of
females were in the workforce, and this figure showed an increase from
the previous decade (United Nations, 1995:26).

The rate of economic activity by women is lower in India than in
most other parts of the world. For example, approximately 60 percent of
the women in East Asia and the former Soviet Union are economically
active, whereas the rate is about 45 to 50 percent in most industrially developed regions such as Europe and North America. About 32 percent of
the women are economically active in Sub-Saharan Africa, Southeast
Asia, Latin America, and the Caribbean. South Asia is only higher than
North Africa and West Asia (United Nations 1991:84).

Although about two-thirds of all main workers in India, defined as
those working at least 183 days per year, are in agriculture-related activities, about 81.2 percent of women workers are employed in this sector,
compared to 63.6 percent of the men. Only 8 percent of women are in the
industrial sector compared to 13.1 percent of the men, whereas 10.8 percent of the women are in the service sector compared to 23.3 percent of
the men. In the agricultural sector, 34.15 percent of main female workers
are classified as cultivators compared to 39.72 percent of the men. However, 44.29 percent of the women are agricultural wage laborers compared to 21.11 percent of the men. Agricultural wage laborers receive
low wages, and the work is often casual and intermittent. Low-caste
Dalit women, in particular, are concentrated in this kind of work, with 71
percent of Dalit women workers being agricultural laborers (Census of
India 1991; Thorat 1998).

The fact that fewer women are cultivators, is related to limits on women's landownership and land use. Although there are a number of examples of communities where women traditionally have had significant rights to land, and women also have acquired rights because of legal reforms, a variety of practical obstacles prevent most women from effectively exercising their rights (Agarwal 1994).

In nonagricultural occupations, men are more likely to find work in the formal sector, and are also more likely than women to be mobile, and have higher educational and vocational skills. Women find more work in the informal sector, and casual work in labor-intensive and low-productivity work. The introduction of new agricultural technologies, such as tractors, threshers, and harvesters, has had a negative impact on women's work. Men are encouraged, and are in a better position, to make use of the new technologies. Women, meanwhile, have seen a reduction in rice-husking and weeding, tasks that were considered women's work.

Women continue to play a significant role in producing handicrafts. But here also, artisans face displacement associated with commercial production. For example, weaving is a family enterprise, with women and men performing separate, but essential tasks. But with increasing competition from mass production of textiles, there is pressure to commercialize and introduce power looms in place of hand looms. Males are better placed than females to make use of the technology and also in marketing products. Women still perform many of the labor-intensive tasks, but are under pressure to produce more and work longer in order to survive. Family obligations as well as patriarchal ideologies allow women's work to be defined as housework, thereby preventing women from demanding higher wages and benefits (Epstein 1996:44–53; Mies 1982).

About 94 percent of the women work in the informal sector of the economy. They are either self-employed or work for low wages. Much of their work is home based, and in a variety of activities, including fisheries, handicrafts, and hand looms, and in small trades, such as making garments and tobacco products, selling vegetables, and so on. And many work as housemaids or become sex workers. In the organized sector, in industrial work, women work in the textile, jute, and mining industries. However, as these industries are declining, women are less likely to find work in the newer industries related to engineering, petrochemicals, fertilizers, and information technology. There has been an increase in women's employment in the service sector of the economy, but most are employed in lower-level clerical and routine jobs.

More salaried, white-collar occupations have opened up for educated middle-class women in urban areas, particularly since the 1970s. Many women do derive some empowerment and satisfaction from these jobs. However, most work out of necessity to support family incomes because inflation continues to be high. Many have little control over their incomes, which often is seen as common family income. Also, women's occupational roles are still considered less important than men's, and women also have primary responsibilities for the family and the household. And often the decision on whether to work in paid employment or not is a family decision rather than an individual one (Desai 1996:97–112; Banerjee 1991).

Many women have, however, challenged traditional family expectations and are working in a variety of nontraditional fields for Indian women, such as the administrative services, banking, sciences, management, and so forth. Middle-class and educated women have also been exposed to many western ideas. Individual family circumstances and experiences interact with the larger social, cultural, and economic trends to determine the actual course taken by individual women.

Women's Education, Fertility, and Mortality

The economic status and well-being of women is closely related to other aspects of women's status, such as education, fertility, and mortality. According to the Census of India, in 1951, 8.86 percent of females were literate, whereas in 1991 the figure had risen to 39.42 percent. Male literacy over the same time period has increased from 27.16 percent to 64.86 percent. Overall, 52 percent of Indians are literate. India is now at about the same level as Sub-Saharan Africa in literacy level (Dreze and Sen 1995:29–31). Most developed countries of Europe and North America and even many developing countries have achieved almost universal literacy for females. In Asia, India's female literacy rate is higher than in Bangladesh and Pakistan, but China (68 percent), South Korea (95 percent), and Thailand (92 percent), for example, have higher rates than India (United Nations 1991:45–46).

However, there are enormous regional variations within India. The state of Kerala in south India has the highest literacy rate in India, at nearly 90 percent, and Bihar has the lowest at 38.5 percent. Female literacy ranges from 86.2 percent in Kerala to 20.4 percent in Rajasthan. In urban areas, however, female literacy is 64 percent compared to male literacy of 81 percent, whereas in rural areas female literacy is 30.62 percent and male literacy is 57.87 percent. The picture is somewhat brighter, however, when we look at literacy levels for girls and boys between the ages of 10 and 14. In 1987–88, 51.7 percent of the girls and 72.9 percent of the boys in rural areas were literate, whereas in urban areas, it was 81.5 percent and 87.9 percent, respectively (Dreze and Sen 1995:218).

As most studies show, lower levels of literacy and education correlate with higher fertility and mortality rates for women, and are related to disadvantages in health and nutrition for females (see, e.g., United Nations 1991). And India is no exception to this trend. The fertility rate in India in 1992 was 3.7 births per woman in 1990, down from 5.7 in 1970. It is, therefore, lower than in Sub-Saharan Africa (6.2) and West Asia (5.3). The fertility rate in India is similar to Latin America and the Caribbean, but higher than in the most developed countries that have a rate of 1.8 (United Nations 1991:60). Within India, the fertility rate is lowest in Kerala at 1.8, and highest in Uttar Pradesh at 5.1. For the most part, states with higher literacy have lower fertility rates (Dreze and Sen 1995:217–18).

Another factor associated with the lower status of women in India is the low female-to-male ratio, which in 1991 stood at 927 females per 1,000 males, down from 972 per 1,000 in 1901 (Dreze and Sen 1995:149). Here again, there are regional variations with the gap being the higher in northwestern and central India, and lower in south India. In fact, in Kerala there are 1,036 females per 1,000 males, and 974 females per 1,000 males in Tamil Nadu, compared to 879 in Uttar Pradesh, 882 in Punjab, 865 in Haryana, and 910 in Rajasthan. Overall, regions with larger gaps in literacy, lower female labor force participation rates, less property rights for women, strong preference for boys, and neglect of girls have higher gaps in female-to-male ratios (Dreze and Sen 1995:140–54).

Although overall life expectancy in India for males and females is 59 years, the mortality rate for girl children under age four is higher than for boys, at 107.4 girls per 100 males. The highest mortality rates are 119 in Rajasthan, 118 in Punjab, 115 in Uttar Pradesh, and 118 in Bihar. At the other end of the spectrum, the female mortality rates for girls are 91 per 100 boys in Kerala, 90 in Tamil Nadu and Andhra Pradesh, and 88 in Himachal Pradesh (Dreze and Sen 1995:220).

This exploration of women's work and social status in India shows that although Indian women face significant disadvantages, there are enormous variations within India. Where concerted state and voluntary efforts have been made to improve social and economic conditions, and women have been engaged in these processes, considerable improvements have been made.

THE INDIAN WOMEN'S MOVEMENT

The Indian women's movement that reemerged in India since the 1970s has taken up a variety of issues related to women's lives and status (Sen 1996; Palriwala and Agnihotri 1996; Gandhi and Shah 1991). It has engaged the state, the patriarchal assumptions underlying state policies and programs, and the traditions that may be disempowering or empowering for women. Although many women had become politically active before independence, after 1950 there was a relative calm in movements against the state until the mid-1960s. A series of economic and political crises, the failure of the state leaders to deliver on their promises, and continuation of many forms of injustice inspired the rise of several protest movements. Women participated in many organizations, especially in many left-wing and socialist organizations mobilizing peasants, workers, and lower castes. They were also active in the antiprice rise movement. Within many of these organizations, there emerged explicit analysis of gender inequality and oppression. In many instances, women's groups within larger organizations formed independent organizations (Sen 1990).

During the 1970s, numerous "autonomous" women's organizations not affiliated with any formal political party were formed, led mainly by middle-class and educated women in the urban areas, and some in rural areas. This happened within the context of the publication in 1974 of *The Report of the Status of Women in India* to commemorate the United Nations International Women's Year in 1975, and the declaration of the state of emergency in India by Prime Minister Indira Gandhi from 1975–77. The number of organizations and issues has continued to grow during the 1980s and 1990s. The organizations have worked on issues such as violence against women, legal reform and redress, education, consciousness-raising, self-help, health and reproductive rights, wages and working conditions, and so on. Many research and documentation centers have also been formed. The women work at many levels, such as lobbying the state, mobilizing on specific issues that arise, and working directly with the women to improve the quality of life. An overview of some key issues and campaigns follows.

Violence against Women

Violence against women is closely related to the subordinate position of women in India, especially as a result of economic exploitation and control of their sexuality. It is reflected in domestic violence, rape, dowry-related harassment, sex determination tests and abortion of female fetuses, female infanticide, and sexual harassment. Women from the upper and middle castes and classes are more likely to experience violence within the family, whereas lower-caste and lower-class women are also more likely to be subjected to violence perpetrated by local landlords, the police, and local political bosses and others in powerful social positions, or by those who use violence to indicate their power (Omvedt 1990).

Women's groups have campaigned against perpetrators of violence, worked on consciousness-raising, and lobbied the government to improve laws and their implementation. In the campaign against rape, for instance, the issue of rape and sexual assault and harassment by the police, the military, rich landlords, upper castes, and so forth, was highlighted. Members of these groups are often in collusion and may prevent effective prosecution of rape cases. As a result of some of these campaigns, there have been some changes in laws relating to handling of rape and violence cases (Gandhi and Shah 1991:39–49).

As will be discussed in Chapter 7, **dowry,** or payment of gifts and cash by the bride's family to the groom and his family at the time of marriage, is a complex phenomenon whose significance and incidence have changed in recent decades. During the 1970s, women's groups focused attention on the harassment of brides and their families by the groom's family if they brought what was considered insufficient dowry at the time of marriage. There was also a noticeable increase in the number of deaths of young married women, usually by burning under suspicious circumstances. These deaths were often registered as accidental or due to suicide. Accurate statistics are difficult to obtain. However, in the late 1980s, an average of two deaths per day of young married women by burning were reported in the Indian capital, Delhi, out of a population of about nine million. And in India's commercial capital, Bombay, 157 cases of burning were reported in a six-month period from September 1987 to February 1988 (Gandhi and Shah 1991:53). In other parts of the country also there was an increase in reports of burnings.

Women's groups mobilized against the groom's family and to raise awareness of the problem. They also set up support centers, and campaigned for tougher laws against dowry, as well as stiffer punishment for those harassing women over dowry. In 1984 the Dowry Prohibition Act was amended to punish those who give or take dowry. However, the definition of dowry is vague and limited, making it easy to sidestep the law. Also, most parents of brides are unlikely to report harassment over the issue for fear of retaliation against their daughters or fear of being punished for giving some dowry in the first place. But if there is a suspicious death of a young married woman, now the laws allow for immediate incarceration of the groom and the in-laws pending trial. The court cases drag on, however, and few charges lead to conviction.

More recently, there is greater realization that legal reforms will not be fully effective unless the subordinate position of girls and daughters within the family is addressed. Women have fewer property rights than males, and do not claim what inheritance rights they do have for fear of creating a rift in the family. And after marriage women are considered to be members of the husband's family. Dowry, then, is often justified as a means to ensure that a daughter has a somewhat higher and more comfortable position in her married home. This, of course, does not always transpire (Gandhi and Shah 1991:54–61).

Female infanticide and sex determination tests that often lead to the abortion of female fetuses are forms of violence that have been taken up recently. During the 19th century, female infanticide was common among some communities, particularly the higher castes, in the northern and central parts of India. It was legally abolished in 1870 as part of the 19th-century reform movements. However, the practice continued surreptitiously among some families. And cases have been reported recently in some villages in northern and southern India (Vishwanath 1996; Karlekar 1998).

Sex determination tests are a more recent development. Ironically, new reproductive technologies developed to monitor the health of the unborn child, such as amniocentesis and ultrasound, are being used to determine the sex of the fetus. This is leading to the abortion of female fetuses among all social classes, particularly the upper and middle classes, in the quest to have male children, especially if the family already has one or two daughters. Reliable statistics are not available, but notes Kishwar (1995a:15) "nearly all of the 15,914 abortions during 1984–85 at a well known abortion clinic in Bombay were undertaken after sex determination tests indicated the fetus was female. Such clinics . . . have sprung up in small towns and villages as well." Other studies reveal similar trends (Karlekar 1998). Campaigns by women's groups and human rights organizations have led to government legislation limiting the performance of these tests except under controlled circumstances. But many are still able to circumvent the law and do not get caught. Female feticide, as well as neglect of little girls, is believed to be a main factor contributing to the lower proportions of females in the Indian population noted earlier, and the gap is expected to widen in the 2001 census (Kishwar 1995b).

Family Law and Gender

As already noted, laws relating to marriage, divorce, property inheritance, child custody, and maintenance are governed by the personal laws of the different religious groups in India. The Government of India has been reluctant to institute the Universal Civil Code relating to families, whereas laws relating to crime, trade, and industry, and so on, are common to all citizens. In terms of family law, however, most Indians are covered under the Hindu Code Bill passed in 1955 and other provisions added over the years because Hindus constitute about 82 percent of the population. Sikhs, Buddhists, and Jains are also covered under the Code. Muslims and Christians are covered by their respective personal laws as defined and interpreted by some of their religious leaders. There are also secular laws in India that cover all Indians, and the Hindu Code generally corresponds with them. Under the Code, the minimum age at marriage is 18 years for females and 21 years for males, **bigamy** is outlawed and divorce has been simplified to make it easier for women to file for divorce. In practice, though, the laws are often violated and enforced only if someone presses charges.

There are several grounds on which Hindu women can ask for divorce, including mutual consent. However, many find it difficult to prove faults such as adultery and cruelty if there is no mutual consent. Most divorce cases continue to be filed by men. The divorce laws also do not cover desertions and bigamous relationships, and it is often impossible to prove bigamy because most people do not register marriages, and there may be various types of non-marital arrangements. Also, there are parallel laws for each religion that often contradict the secular civil laws. Under the Indian Divorce Act of 1869 covering Christians, women have to prove adultery, bigamy, and cruelty in order to obtain a divorce. Men only have to prove adultery. There have been some recent efforts to change these inequities (Gandhi and Shah 1991:252–67). However, the divorce rate remains very low in India, although it is rising, especially in urban areas. In the late 1980s, only 0.8 percent of women between the ages of 25 and 44 were divorced in India, compared to between 4 and 12 percent in most European and North American countries (United Nations 1991:26–29).

Most controversy, however, has centered around Muslim Personal Law as practiced in India, which covers the 12 percent of the Indian population that is Muslim. Muslim Personal Law is very complex and varied, but overall males have more rights and powers under it than females. For example, it is easier for a man to obtain a divorce than for a female. And a female has to be supported financially by her own family if divorced or unmarried. A few Muslim women have come forward to challenge the ways in which Muslim Personal Law has been formulated and interpreted by Muslim clerics and conservative Muslims in India. In 1983, Shehnaaz Sheikh argued with the Supreme Court of India that the Muslim Personal Law violated her constitutional rights as an Indian citizen. However, she modified her petition and demanded revision, rather than a repeal, of the Muslim Personal Law in keeping with both the Qur'an and the Indian Constitution (Gandhi and Shah 1991:235–37).

Much more contentious has been the case of Shah Bano, an elderly Muslim woman who asked for maintenance from her divorced husband under the Indian Civil Code in 1985. The Indian Supreme Court granted her maintenance, and in the process criticized the Muslim Personal Law as biased. This led to widespread protests by many Muslim groups. They viewed the Supreme Court verdict as an attack on the fundamental tenets of Islam. Other Muslims argued that Muslim law was very egalitarian and did not need to be changed. The Congress-led Indian government, meanwhile, introduced the Muslim Women's Bill in Parliament upholding the Muslim Personal Law. The Muslims form a significant vote-bank in electoral politics in many parts of India, and until then the majority of Muslims had supported the Congress. The Bharatiya Janata Party, drawing most of its support from conservative Hindus, opposed the Muslim Women's Bill in Parliament. Many women's organizations also opposed the Bill. Some progressive Muslim women's groups, such

as the Committee for the Protection of Rights of Muslim Women, also argued that the right of a Muslim woman to maintenance upon divorce did
not constitute a violation of the rights of Muslims as a minority. Under
the pressure of the controversy, and not wanting to create a rift within
her community, Shah Bano withdrew her case (Hasan 1998).

Underlying this controversy is the debate on whether to have a
Uniform Civil Code, and on how to balance it while allowing freedom
of religion. Many progressive activists and middle-class intellectuals,
including women, argue for instituting the UCC as a step toward
equality and social justice for all individuals. Many conservative and
right-wing Hindu leaders also support the UCC, but on the basis of
their argument that India is first and foremost a Hindu nation and any
"concessions" to minorities are viewed as a sign of weakness in the fabric of Indian society and culture. Many Muslims, meanwhile, charge
that the UCC is really a Hindu code that is sought to be imposed on
non-Hindus.

There is also considerable debate over the issue within the Indian
women's movement. Many Indian middle-class feminists want the UCC
to be instituted as a key mechanism toward greater equality and social
justice for women in their families and communities. However, they
have not yet found an effective way to challenge the personal laws. They
also realize that religion is an important source of identity and strength
for women as well as men. Also, the Hindu right-wing movement has
managed to garner the support of many women in the cause of India as a
Hindu nation by idealizing the role of the virtuous Hindu Indian woman
as the key element of a strong Indian culture and society (Jeffery and
Basu 1998).

Some women activists argue for more dialogues on the meaning of
the religious personal laws among women from all religions. Many state
that a fair and just UCC should be formulated, and all women should
have the option of demanding their rights under the UCC if they believe
the personal laws to be discriminatory. This is viewed as a compromise,
but the assumption is that if more women are assisted in resorting to the
UCC, there would be an impetus to change the personal laws in a more
egalitarian direction (Gandhi and Shah 1991; Kishwar 1993, 1995b).

Activists are aware, however, that changes in formal laws alone
will not transform patriarchal relations within the family and society.
Women often do not claim their rights so as not to cause discord within
the family, or there may not be viable alternatives for them. Many
women also may be unaware of the laws, and others do not perceive the
laws to be egalitarian and don't trust the legal system.

Several grassroots women's organizations have emerged to focus on
documenting laws, legal education, reform, and consciousness-raising. In
some instances, women's groups have set up alternative institutions in the
communities, such as the **Mahila Panchayats** or women's councils in four

urban communities in Delhi. Women from the communities and trained activists are dealing with a variety of issues such as violence, dowry, marital problems, property disputes, and they assist in resolving disputes at the community level. They also assist in obtaining legal counsel if cases have to be taken to the formal legal system (Sekhon 1999).

Other Issues and Actions

Numerous women's organizations have taken on the complex issue of women's health. Women's health is related to social and cultural factors, such as gender inequality and lack of power within the family; lack of control over fertility, poverty, and related problems such as poor nutrition; overwork; poor working conditions; lack of access to health services; and silence over issues related to sexuality. Government and international agencies have tended to focus on introduction of reproductive technologies in order to reduce the number of births, but without challenging the inegalitarian social and cultural conditions that undermine the effectiveness of their programs. Women's groups have focused on education and awareness about preventive health, reproductive health, and various forms of birth control. Many provide access to medical services, and also focus on social and economic empowerment of women as an important part of improving their health.

One example is the Community Health Worker program of the Comprehensive Rural Health Program (CRHP) started in 1971 in the village of Jamkhed in Maharashtra. Women from Jamkhed and other villages were recruited and trained to deal with diagnosis and treatment of several health and nutrition issues. However, they also incorporated environmental projects such as reforestation and sanitation, and over the years the caste and gender hierarchies were also challenged and overturned (Arcaro 1992). Similarly, Action India, an organization working with women, young girls, and children in four low-income communities in Delhi, initiated a Community Health Worker program in 1984, that has grown to focus on reproductive health, fertility consciousness, self-help, and herbal medicine. Recognizing the social and economic factors that relate to health, they have started related programs for economic empowerment, alternative legal services, and consciousness-raising and action through the *Sabla Sanghs,* or association of empowered women, and forums for young girls and children in the communities (Sekhon 1999).

Women have also been active in movements to acquire land rights, better wages and working conditions, and protecting forests and the environment. Several organizations, such as the Self Employed Women's Association (SEWA) and Women's Working Forum (WWF), have become successful in assisting women with access to credit in order to improve their economic conditions. Alongside economic empowerment, however, they also assist with issues of health, family planning, child care, financial management, legal assistance, and so forth.

Many of these actions are directed at the state, whereas others work to develop programs alternative to the state. Many women's groups have initiated debates on traditions with a view to uncovering the diversities in India's past and present. This becomes a means to acknowledge those aspects of Indian culture that are empowering, and those that are oppressive, leading to the possibility of change toward a more egalitarian society. The overall impact of the work of numerous women's groups is difficult to assess. Change is often slow and the results contradictory. However, many networks and coalitions have also emerged to take on particular policy issues and campaigns. The various groups working at several levels on different issues also come together every two years for the National Conference of Women's Movements to share ideas, assess their work, analyze issues, and affirm their objectives. Increasingly, over the last two decades, Indian political leaders and state institutions have been compelled to take more explicit note of the issues affecting women and girls. They have also had to deal with issues of representation of women in formal political institutions of society, as discussed in the next section.

WOMEN AND FORMAL POLITICS

Women's representation in formal political parties and elected bodies at the national, state, and local levels has remained very low until recently. Many women participated in the nationalist movement. And after independence there have been a few prominent women in Indian politics, most notably, Indira Gandhi, who was India's prime minister for all but four years between 1967 and 1984. She and many other women in politics were inspired by their connections with male family members who were active in politics, although some did go on to develop a political base of their own. Overall, however, the number of women in Parliament has remained very low, approximately 5 percent, rising to 8 percent in the 1998 elections. The percentage of women in most state assemblies is even lower. Although most women's groups that emerged during the 1970s and 1980s stayed away from electoral politics, many did campaign for more representation of women and women's issues in political institutions. Consequently, many government policies explicitly dealt with women's issues, and political parties addressed women's issues in their electoral platforms (Kumar 1995b:59–72).

By the late 1980s, debate started on whether to reserve seats in various elected bodies for women, similar to reservation for the scheduled castes, tribes, and other backward classes. The issue of women's

representation emerged alongside calls for more autonomy for local political institutions. Traditional village and town councils known as **Panchayats** existed in India before British rule, and were revived in many
states after independence. But no real power was delegated to them,
and no regular elections were held. After considerable debate, the Indian Parliament passed the 73rd amendment to the Constitution in
1992, known as the Panchayati Raj Bill, or "rule of the local councils."
An important provision of the Bill was the reservation of 33 percent of
all seats in local Panchayats for women. Already in some states, such as
Maharashtra, some peasant-based organizations, such as the Shetkari
Sangathan, had already put up female candidates in local elections
since the mid-1980s, and several of them had been elected, including
all-women Panchayats. With the passing of the Panchayati Raj Bill, several states started elections to local bodies in 1994, and by late 1996
about one million women had been elected to various self-governing
local institutions (Datta 1998; Dhillon and Baweja 1996).

In spite of many tensions, conflicts, and problems, early evidence
points to dramatic changes in social and political structure in many parts
of India. There is widespread skepticism and disbelief on the part of
men, but many have actively supported women. Many females, however, are wives or relatives of locally powerful men. They are often illiterate, tied to traditional family roles, and with little experience in public
affairs. And many are from middle- and upper-caste families, or with
links to corrupt politicians. However, a number of women have developed political skills, worked hard to learn their roles and responsibilities,
and developed independent political agenda. They have turned to focus
on issues such as clean and safe drinking water, health, education, job
training, land rights for women and lower castes, stopping licenses for
the sale of liquor, and accountability on the part of government officials
and bureaucrats. Several women also express a greater sense of empowerment, awareness, and knowledge; greater freedom of mobility; more
power within the family; and more respect and recognition in the community. Most of the women elected so far are married and older, with
fewer child-rearing and related responsibilities. However, more recently,
several younger women are also emerging to show an interest in local affairs. Several organizations, such as Aalochana Centre for Documentation and Research on Women in the city of Pune in western India, are developing and conducting training programs to prepare women for
effective participation in the Panchayats (Singh et al. 1992; Joshi 1995;
Times of India 1997).

This process has ignited debate on the issue of reservation of seats
in elections to state legislatures and the Parliament for women. Strong ar-
guments have been made both for and against reservation of seats. Most
of the bigger political parties, especially the BJP, the Congress, and the
Left Front, have come out in favor of reservation in principle. However,

Women attending a training camp to enable participation in Panchayats in the village of Brahmangarh in Pune District (Maharashtra). The women pictured here are discussing their vision of an ideal village community. Photo by Lalita Joshi *(Courtesy: Aalochana Centre for Documentation and Research on Women).*

whenever the Reservation Bill has been introduced into Parliament, first in 1996 and then in July and December 1998, there has been enormous controversy, and the measure has not been passed. Those favoring the Bill argue that this is the only way to ensure adequate representation of women. Others argue that most women so elected will be those with connections to male politicians, and those from middle and upper castes and classes. A key debate now is on the issue of reserving some women's constituencies for women from the lower castes and tribes, and the Other Backward Classes (OBCs). Opponents also argue that once seats are reserved for women, there will be no effort made to elect women from other constituencies. Also, reservation would prevent men from being elected from some areas. Some suggest rotation of constituencies reserved for women. However, that will prevent a candidate from building a strong support base over a period of time and may interfere with the work she or he may do for the area. The issue, therefore, is very complex, and a reasonable solution will be difficult to attain. But it is indicative of the importance of the gender dynamics in India that the issue is being debated so hotly.

CONCLUSION

Gender roles and relationships in India have for centuries been part of an active public discourse. The role of women in the maintenance of social status has always been integral to any understanding of Indian culture. It is not surprising, therefore, to see so many literary texts devoted to the appropriate roles and responsibilities of women. Debates over these issues point to the variety in women's roles and status in different parts of India and among different castes and classes. Movements to improve the position of women have taken on and redefined issues related to gender in the Indian context. The issue of gender in India cannot be discussed only from the point of view of women's subordinate status. We also need to look at the numerous debates, and some real changes and improvements in women's lives in India. And the issue of gender equality is impacted not only by patriarchal social structures, but also economic structures and processes that limit social and economic equality.

CHAPTER 7

Family Diversity and Education

A matrimonial advertisement in the "Bridegrooms Wanted" section of a Sunday newspaper in North India states: "Wanted IPS (Indian Police Service), IAS (Indian Administrative Service), IRS (Indian Revenue Service), Bank Officer, engineer, well-settled businessman for very beautiful fair, slim, convent educated Brahman girl, 24/5'-2", M.Sc. (Food and Nutrition), belonging to a well-connected highly educated prestigious family, having vast agricultural land. Early and decent marriage." Another advertisement in the "Brides Wanted" section reads: "Jat Sikh parents seeking suitable match for their Canadian Citizen handsome and brilliant 5' 8" tall, 26-year-old son with a Bachelor of Mathematics and Computer Science and professionally employed. Girl should be beautiful, tall, intelligent with good nature and education (B.Sc. minimum with fluent English) and belong to respectable family. Please respond with returnable photograph. Boy visiting India early August."

These advertisements clearly illustrate the significance of family background, status, and education in arranging marriages in contemporary India. They stand in sharp contrast to the personal advertisements in American newspapers, one of which states: "Not willing to give up! Very young, attractive, financially/emotionally secure, playful, humorous, intelligent, easygoing, responsible SWPM, 43, 5'10", 175 pounds, nonsmoker. Seeking sweet, sincere, attractive, fun-loving SWF for wining, dining, romance, adventure and possible LTR (long-term relationship)."

These advertisements highlight the differences in family ties, and marital and intimate relationships between India and North America. And North Americans, socialized to think of romantic love as the basis of long-term relationships and marriage, express an enormous amount of curiosity about some features of Indian families, and find it difficult to comprehend marriages arranged by families in India. Many westerners and Indians also marvel at what appears to be strong family ties in India expressed through family loyalty, obligations, and responsibilities. These features, however, coexist with conflicts and tensions over roles, relationships, and responsibilities. Moreover, in India, as elsewhere, idealized visions of family life are often confused with actual experiences of individual families shaped by their unique circumstances. Furthermore, social, cultural, economic, demographic and political changes have modified family ideals and traditions in significant ways.

In this chapter we will look at beliefs, values, and norms concerning marriage, location of residence, descent, and authority within the family that affect the nature of kinship ties, as well as the lives of individual family members. This will be followed by a consideration of gender, patriarchy, household structure, socialization, as well as state policies affecting families within the context of social and economic change. Finally, we will assess the role and structure of education in modern India, as well as diversities in the Indian educational system that are fundamentally related to family status.

MARRIAGE RULES AND ARRANGEMENTS

An overwhelming majority of marriages in India are arranged by families rather than by the individuals themselves. Marriage is seen as an institution that creates a social bond between two families rather than two individuals. It is, therefore, an important medium through which social status is reflected, maintained, and even enhanced. As is apparent from the matrimonial advertisements quoted above, considerations of caste, occupation, economic position, as well as religion and language are believed to be significant factors in ensuring a good marriage. These social and cultural similarities, it is believed and hoped, will lead to a harmonious relationship between the married couple and their respective families. Romantic love is not considered to be a secure basis for marriage although it is idealized in the popular culture and several myths.

On the surface, this is a dramatically different method of arranging marriages than in the Western hemisphere. But when we look at the actual outcome of marriages in the West and determine who marries whom, the differences do not appear that dramatic after all. Although there have been some changes in recent years, nearly all Americans marry or enter into long-term relationships with people of the same race as themselves. Americans are more likely to marry others of a similar religion, social class, educational level, and location as themselves. There are also unwritten and written rules governing dating and marriage. For instance, the expectation is that individuals date someone of a similar age and that a romantic or marital relationship should be with a person of the opposite sex. For the most part, however, these norms and rules have been internalized and appear as choices being made by individuals. The role of families as agents of socialization is more subtle in the West when compared to the explicit role of families in enforcing marriage rules in India. However, arranged marriages vary both in terms of rules concerning marriage, as well as the manner in which arrangements are made.

The actual rules of marriage vary by region, caste, religion, class, and individual family circumstances, and have changed continuously. However, there are also some common normative ideals that frame kinship ties. Historically, in northern India the dominant norm among Hindus, who constitute about 82 percent of the population, is to marry outside the clan, or descent group, of the father and the mother. Related to this is the norm of village **exogamy.** Arranging a marriage with a person from a village at some distance is also a way to ensure clan exogamy. Actual rules and practices with respect to how far back to go into the descent line before a marriage can be arranged vary considerably, and the rules have become more flexible in recent times. The ideal remains, however, that people related closely by blood should not marry. Descent is traced along **patrilineal** lines, and the residential pattern is **patrilocal,** that is, upon marriage the bride moves to live with the groom and his family in his village. This move marks a clear break with the bride's natal family, and she then becomes a member of her husband's family. Traditionally, there are restrictions on visiting between the bride and her family, but again these restrictions are variable and changing (Karve 1993 [1953]:54–56).

The status of the wife-giving family is lower than that of the wife takers, corresponding to the lower status of females in a **patriarchal** society. This status differential is reflected in many parts of northern India through the practice of **hypergamy,** according to which a woman is married to a man from a higher-status family but usually within the same caste. For a man to marry a woman of a lower status is not a problem as family status derives from the status of the husband/father. Several examples of hypergamy are to be found mainly among the upper castes, such as the Kulin Brahmans in Bengal, Anavil Brahmans of Gujarat, and among the Kshatriya groups, such as the Marathas, Rajputs, and Patidars. The practice has been modified, but not ended, with modern and Western influences. The desire to raise status through marriage to a person of higher status remains. However, status is now determined more by education and economic and occupational standing within the larger caste group (Uberoi 1993:230–32).

In southern India, there is a distinct preference for cross-cousin marriages and uncle-niece marriages. For example, marriage is arranged between children of siblings of the opposite sex. Thus, a man may marry his father's sister's daughter or the mother's brother's daughter. A woman may marry her mother's younger brother, although usually not the mother's older brother. And although a woman becomes a member of her husband's family, she does not usually live very far away from her natal family, and there are fewer restrictions on meeting and visiting. In actual practice, however, uncles and cousins of the appropriate age may not be available, their horoscopes according to Hindu traditions may not match, and there may be other reasons why a marriage may not be considered appropriate. There is also some evidence that these practices are declining in recent years.

Common to marriage practices among Hindus in most parts of northern and southern India is the idea and practice of **kanyadaan** or the gift of the daughter by her father to the husband and his family. The practice of kanyadaan is connected to the higher status accorded to wife-takers over wife-givers, and is believed to have originated among the Indo-Aryans and then spread among the Dravidians to the south. The higher status of the groom's family is expressed through numerous rituals of gift giving by the bride's family before marriage, at the time of marriage, and after marriage on occasions such as births and deaths.

The higher status of the groom and his family is related to patrilineal descent, patrilocal residence, and the higher status of males. In most parts of India, however, the higher castes and those groups who desire to raise their social status place a greater emphasis on patrilineal lineage and patrilocal residence. In a village in the western Indian state of Gujarat, for example, the lineage structure was stronger among the land-owning Rajputs than among the other castes in 1825. By 1955, there was stronger emphasis on lineage among the Rajputs, but also among the lower castes. The latter developed genealogies in order to claim a higher status (Madan 1993 [1975]). In the South Indian village of Tanjore also, lineage ties and patrilocal residential patterns are stronger among the Brahmans than among the lower castes (Gough 1993 [1956]). Ownership of land makes it more important among the dominant castes to maintain a patrilineal lineage structure to ensure proper inheritance of property and transmission of status.

In some castes and tribes in India descent is traced along the female lineage. However, **matrilineal** descent does not necessarily ensure greater authority for females in society, although their status within the family often tends to be higher than among patrilineal descent groups. Among the Khasis in northeastern India, for example, women inherit property. But they also bear and rear children, and are the keepers of family honor and virtue. Men are, therefore, viewed as protectors of women and their assistance is seen as important. They have a lot of control and authority over decisions, and more freedom in public life outside the family. With the conversion of many Khasis to Christianity and other modern influences, the system of matrilineal descent and inheritance is becoming weaker, and there are fears of an increase in gender inequality in favor of males (Nongbri 1993 [1988]). Influence of the dominant patrilineal system of descent and patriarchal authority is also having a negative influence on many other hitherto matrilineal tribes.

The variety in marriage and kinship systems in India is also reflected in the example of the Nayars, a non-Brahman caste, in the southern Indian state of Kerala. Exhibiting a matrilineal descent system, Nayar women married both Nayar men and/or entered into a form of marriage with Nambudiri Brahman men. These marriages or marriage-like arrangements were often polygamous. Nayar women lived in households composed of members tracing descent through women, and husbands usually did not live with their wives. From the point of view of the Nambudiri men, these relationships were often not viewed as marriages, but from the point of view of the Nayar women, the Nambudiri men were their husbands. When children of such unions were born, however, the children were granted legitimacy as belonging to the father's caste and lineage (Gough 1993 [1959]).

Polygamy was much more widespread in many parts of India in the past. It was outlawed after independence, but still continues, though it is not clear to what extent. Also legal action cannot be taken to enforce the law unless the spouses object to the arrangement. A man married more than one wife (**polygyny**) often if the first wife could not have a child. There are also several examples of **polyandry,** particularly among some tribes in the Himalayan region in the North. The ideal was when a woman was married to the eldest brother and then became a wife of all the other brothers in the household. It is important to keep in mind, though, that in the same caste or tribe, polygamy was never the only form of marital arrangement. Monogamy was practiced and often in the same family more than one type of marital arrangement was exhibited at different stages of a lifetime (Berreman 1993 [1975]).

Though Islamic personal law based on the **Sharia** is recognized as the guiding principle of the Muslim family and kinship structure, the regional and local cultural environment affects actual practices. There are, therefore, several similarities in marital arrangements among Hindus and Muslims, although the content of the ceremonies may be different. And although polygamy is allowed under Muslim law, it is not widely practiced. Among the Muslims there is also a tendency to arrange marriages among close relatives as in southern India (Ahmed 1976).

Given that individual choice and romantic love as the basis of marriage are not conducive to the maintenance of rules of caste, status, and lineage, most marriages continue to be arranged. There is, however, more variability and flexibility now than in the past, particularly in urban areas. The prospective bride and groom often meet and get acquainted before their marriage, and many are able to express their preferences, even though they may face varying degrees of pressure and persuasion from their families. In urban areas, although there may be less concern now over maintenance of caste and complex kinship rules, there is a great emphasis on class and socioeconomic status. Most young people are socialized to accept arranged marriages as the norm. And even when individuals find rules to be restrictive, they often view them to be inevitable. A dating system like the one in North America is not prevalent. However, couples are also beginning to develop closer emotional ties with one another, even as they maintain family obligations and responsibilities. And many incorporate romantic love ideals into their relationships.

GENDER, PATRIARCHY, AND THE FAMILY

Dominant practices relating to marriage reflect a patriarchal family system. Although there have been some changes and greater flexibility in recent years, the family dynamics summarized here continue to be dominant especially among the middle- and upper-status castes and classes. Typically, the oldest male member of the family has the most authority and the highest status. Younger brothers and sons are expected to defer to the wishes of the older males. Children are under the authority of the parents, particularly the father.

But the key to the maintenance of the family and kinship system is the regulation of gender relations. Through marriage a woman becomes a member of her husband's family. As a daughter-in-law she has little authority within the family. However, a woman is valued as a mother, and her status rises when she has children, especially if she has sons. She experiences a further rise in status when a daughter-in-law enters the household upon the marriage of her son, if she has one. The wife also has primary responsibility for performing household tasks. She and her husband are not expected to display overt affection for one another. A daughter is more privileged and freer to move around than a daughter-in-law, but she has less freedom of movement than a son. And a son's education is considered more important than a daughter's. A daughter's upbringing is conditioned by the fact that she is to be married appropriately. There is also a greater degree of control over female sexuality than male sexuality. When resources are limited, there is more neglect of the girl child than of a boy. On the whole, males get preference in food, nutrition, health care, and education, and the mortality rate is higher for females than for males.

Even when a wife works, she has less control over her income. Her income is usually viewed as supplementing the household income, whereas the husband is viewed as the primary breadwinner, and he usually is in a higher paying job. Many women, however, have experienced changes in consciousness as a result of education, other modern influences, and also the women's movement. They also have greater influence within the household. Changes in women's consciousness, however, are not often matched by corresponding changes in men's consciousness and roles, leading to tensions and conflicts. It is important to keep in mind, though, that many women express satisfaction with their lives within the family. Also women's status within the family does change over a period of time, and they do acquire greater authority as they become older (Seymour 1994 & 1999; Ullrich 1994).

However, gender hierarchy is more strongly apparent among the higher-status castes than among the lower castes. For example, Gough (1993 [1956]) found that in a South Indian village, a lower-economic status associated with lack of landownership means that the labor of women is more important. They are, therefore, more economically independent and have a more equal relationship with their husbands. Residential patterns are also more flexible, with men often living in villages of their mothers or wives. And sons are less dependent on their fathers for their livelihood. Women's sexuality is less restricted than among the upper-status castes, and they have closer ties with their own natal family. Seymour (1999:145–57) in her study of a rapidly urbanizing state capital also found less subservience to husbands, less gender segregation in household tasks, more informality, flexibility, and cooperation among family members among the working-class, poor, and lower-caste households.

The differential status of males and females is reflected in a fundamental way in the forms of payments and gifts made at the time of marriage. Traditionally, two main forms of marriage payments existed in India and they reflect the status of wife-givers relative to wife-takers. **Bride wealth** or **bride price** was paid by the groom's family to the bride's family. This was because a bride was believed to add wealth to the groom's family in the form of labor and reproduction of children. The payment was made to compensate the bride's family for their loss. This practice was more characteristic of lower-status families, particularly in southern India. More common among the upper-status groups, and particularly in northern India, is the form of marriage payment termed **dowry.** Dowry takes various forms and includes gifts made to the groom and his family in relation to the marriage, and gifts to the bride to set up her conjugal household. She gives up rights to a share in the parental property, and is not believed to add wealth to the husband's household in the form of labor.

Over the course of the 20th century, dowry has become more widespread among middle- and lower-status groups, and has also become more widespread in the South. This reflects the spread of the Indo-Aryan influence from the north to the south, as well as a desire among lower-status groups to raise their status by acquiring ritual traditions associated with higher castes. The rise of the dowry is also related to the rise of commercialism and consumerism as part of the process of modernization and industrialization. Acquisition of consumer goods has emerged as an important status symbol, and dowry becomes a means to acquire these goods. Some studies show that even when women are educated and earning a wage, the amount of dowry that is expected from their families is not reduced by much. Moreover, dowry is also spreading among Christians (Srinivas 1984; Sharma 1993 [1984]; Caplan 1993 [1984]). But as expenses go up along with economic changes, in many working and middle-class families, the education and earning potential of the wife may override dowry considerations, as some recent studies show (Mukhopadhyay and Seymour 1994; Seymour 1999).

Although some form of dowry is widespread in India, it is not something that is always explicitly discussed when a marriage is arranged. This is because of several laws and movements against dowry in recent years, as well as the fact that the groom's family does not want to appear to be greedy. However, the laws are inadequate and contain numerous loopholes, and are difficult to enforce. And every effort is made to make it appear as though the bride's family is willingly making a choice in giving dowry. Many feminists and others working to bring about gender equity believe that the only way for the dowry system to end is to raise the status of women and view them as assets rather than as liabilities. This would also mean a fundamental change in the system of kanyadaan under which a Hindu bride is given away by her father to her husband.

HOUSEHOLD STRUCTURE AND SOCIAL CHANGE

Considerable attention has been paid to changes in family and house-hold structure as a result of social changes associated with modernization, industrialization, and urbanization. It is commonly believed that the traditional Indian family is characterized by a **joint family** household and **extended family** ties. Many also believe that the traditional Indian family is changing as a result of social and economic trends and is giving way to the **nuclear family** system. Reality in the past and present, however, remains much more complex. Ideally, a joint family consists of a household in which one or two married couples live with their married sons, unmarried children, and/or grandchildren. They share close kinship ties, place expectations upon one another, are obligated to perform roles necessary for the maintenance of the family. They may also share extended family ties with other close relatives not living in the same household, and provide financial support and other assistance. The term "joint family" is sometimes applied to a group of related adults owning property jointly, but living in separate households (Uberoi 1993:384; Madan 1993 [1976]:419–21).

Recent studies do show some changes in the nature of family ties and household structure, but the direction of these changes is not uniform or unilinear. And there is no clear evidence of a significant decline in joint family households, and a corresponding increase in nuclear family households. Many studies show that there has in fact been an increase in the proportion of joint family households in rural and many urban areas when compared to earlier in the 20th century. For example, in the village of Karimpur in the northern Indian state of Uttar Pradesh, Wadley and Derr (1993 [1988]) found many different household types. These include single-person households, nuclear family households, joint family households, subnuclear families (a part of a former nuclear family), and supplemented nuclear family (nuclear family with one or more relatives of the parents), and other variations of those mentioned here. Between 1925 and 1984, there was an increase in the number of both nuclear and joint family households, but a decline in subnuclear and supplemented nuclear family households. Because of lower life expectancy in earlier years, there were not as many adults living to comprise a joint family in the strict sense of the term. The higher-status families with large landholdings are more likely to have joint families in Karimpur when compared to those with less land or no land.

Overall, the joint family remains a cultural ideal and is believed to be an indicator of family strength and unity. Urbanization and industrialization have not significantly affected the ideal. Often, though, practical considerations affect the actual household structure. Once the household reaches a certain size, some of the sons or grandsons may form nuclear households. These nuclear households may then develop into joint family households when their sons marry and stay in the household. Mobility associated with new occupational opportunities may also lead to the formation of nuclear family households, as well as subnuclear or supplemented nuclear family households. However, even when members of a family form separate households, they retain varying degrees of kinship ties and obligations. These include financial responsibility, participation in family rituals on various occasions, help in finding jobs, care of older parents, provision of contacts and connections to ensure social mobility, and so forth.

Urbanization has been slow in India when compared to many other less-developed countries, with only about 25 percent of the population living in urban areas. Many of the people in urban areas are migrants from the villages in search of livelihood, and this migration is usually a family decision. Often a male family member moves alone, or may bring his wife and children along. However, he still maintains close ties to the village, visits as frequently as possible, and maintains financial and other obligations toward his parents, brothers, and sisters. Other family members, such as brothers, sisters, uncles, aunts, nieces, and nephews, may follow the first migrant to the city, and many relatives may live in the same household for varying periods of time (Vatuk 1989). Even among members of a Dalit caste, who usually exhibit a more varied household structure in the rural settings, the key ideal is the joint family in their squatter settlement in Delhi (Haider 1997a).

Among those engaged in the modern bureaucratic occupations, however, some changes are evident in urban areas (Vatuk 1989; Seymour 1999). There is more freedom and flexibility for the young and for women, although this varies according to individual families. And married couples are freer to express emotional intimacy. However, there are also certain aspects of urban family life that cause stress in family relationships. For instance, lack of support from extended kin makes it more difficult to take care of needs of children, and there are more pressures on the married couple to take care of various family obligations. Economic stress, as well as the organization of work that requires extended hours away from other family members, often leads to strained family relationships. The sons still bear the primary responsibility for their older parents, and it is usually the daughter-in-law who takes care of a lot of practical responsibilities in this regard.

These stresses are linked to an increase in divorce, particularly in the urban areas, although the divorce rate is still very low. Officially, less than 1 percent of women and men between the ages of 15 and 44 are divorced, although many believe that a greater number are separated or do not report a divorce because of the stigma attached to it. No one keeps statistics, but anecdotal evidence points to an increase in divorce particularly in urban areas. By comparison, about 10 percent of women in the United States report being divorced (Amato 1994).

SOCIALIZATION

In India, as elsewhere, individuals learn the appropriate values and norms of the social group through the process of **socialization.** They learn ideals and expectations such as family loyalty, solidarity, as well as age and gender differentiation, even if they are not able to live according to these values and norms. Socialization practices vary according to family social and economic circumstances. And as children grow up, a variety of educational, economic, and other experiences and circumstances may alter lives and aspirations.

Traditionally and ideally, Indian children grow up in the presence of several adults, siblings, and cousins, and others within the joint family or community. Until about age five or six their physical needs such as feeding and cleaning are met on demand, and there are few explicit rules of discipline. However, parents make clear that they have authority over the children and decide how the children's needs are met. Children are ordered to perform tasks, are expected to obey, and are given few rewards and little praise, and it is not considered appropriate to show too much overt affection. This pattern is more apparent in rural areas. Seymour (1999:70–85) also found this pattern among many middle- and upper-status families, often living in joint households, in the older section of Bhubaneshwar, the capital of the state of Orissa. Children are taught the value of interdependence as part of the family unit rather than independence from the family.

After about age six, however, girls and boys are prepared for gender-differentiated roles and behaviors. Girls are prepared for eventual marriage, and the role of daughter-in-law, wife, and mother. They are taught household tasks, and are prepared to adjust to conditions in the in-laws' home. Boys are prepared to be educated and become responsible heads of households. A variety of rituals, ceremonies, and folk sayings reinforce the importance of males for family well-being, and the lower status of females in the household (Dube 1988).

This pattern of socialization varies somewhat among those families in urban areas that are more incorporated into newer Western-oriented education and professional or bureaucratic occupations, as well as among upwardly mobile families in rural areas. Socialization of children is more child centered, and there is more individual attention, nurturing, and focus on promoting developmental skills through stimulating activities and tutoring. Although family responsibilities are considered important, the focus is on self-reliance and independence (see e.g., Seymour 1999:125–44). There is more stress on education for both boys and girls, although for boys the goal of education is to prepare for a career, and for girls, a certain level of education is considered necessary in order to obtain a suitable man to marry.

Among the poorer households, however, adults have to work hard to meet family needs, and are, therefore, less available to meet the physical and emotional needs of the children. Children learn to be self-reliant early, and are often cared for by a variety of adults, siblings, and other relatives. Mothers tend to perform various chores while feeding children, for example. Girls do perform more household tasks than boys, and educational opportunities are limited, although considered more important for males.

THE STATE AND THE FAMILY

The Indian state has also been an active player in advocating a strong family as the backbone of a strong Indian society. However, the desire to be a modern, progressive, and egalitarian society is often at odds with the desire to preserve what are viewed as cultural traditions transmitted through a strong and united family that frequently have inegalitarian consequences for different members of the family.

The official Indian state perspective on the family is encapsulated in the *Indian Approach Paper for the International Year of the Family in 1994* (Uberoi 1996). The Paper extols the strength and unity of the Indian family, while also stressing the role of the state in democratizing the family by challenging patriarchal structures and attitudes that perpetuate gender and age inequalities. There is also a recognition of the connection between oppression and inequities within the family, and various forms of social and economic deprivations, especially in the areas of nutrition, health, and education. The state, therefore, acknowledges its role in providing resources, and ensuring equality of access, so that the needs of children, girls, and women are adequately addressed. A variety of policies have been instituted to address these issues, but the implementation has been partial and uneven, and consequences have been contradictory. The role of the state in relation to the family is best illustrated through some state laws relating to families and India's population control policies that are officially termed "family planning" policies.

As already discussed in the previous chapter, certain aspects of family life, such as marriage, divorce, maintenance, and property inheritance, are governed by the personal laws of the different religious groups in India. And in these personal laws males have greater rights than females. The Government of India did bring about some modifications in Hindu personal law, such as outlawing polygamy, granting women the right to adopt, and giving them more property rights. However, women still have fewer rights than men. And even with more egalitarian laws, enforcement is limited to cases that are brought before the courts, and in most instances women are unable or unwilling to enforce the laws.

The Indian government has sought to control population growth ever since independence through its "family planning" policies. While policy makers sought to encourage families to voluntarily limit the number of children born, they also hoped that economic development and modernization would inevitably lead to a decline in the birth rate as in many more industrialized parts of the world. However, in the first three decades after independence, the population increased at an even faster rate than before independence, averaging about 2 percent per year, neutralizing many of the gains of economic development.

Government-sponsored family planning and population control policies became more aggressive, encouraged by support from international agencies such as the United Nations. The focus of these policies has been on limiting the number of births. The main strategy has been to promote various forms of birth control, mainly sterilization, but also contraceptive use. Women are the main focus of these programs. Indeed, fertility rates have declined from about 5.7 births per woman in the 1960s to 3.7 by 1991, and are expected to drop even further. And the population growth rate is expected to drop below 1 percent per year in the next two decades.

Critics, particularly members of women's organizations, charge, however, that the family planning programs assume women are free to make choices and have autonomy within their families. There continues to be widespread preference for sons over daughters. As a result, women are compelled to produce sons or have internalized the desire to do so. Women may also lack full information on issues of reproductive health or access to adequate health services. The government, however, has not addressed the issue of lack of access to resources, and the unequal distribution of power within the family. And although the rate of population growth is slowing, India's population is not expected to stabilize until the second half of the 21st century.

Under pressure from many women's groups and also as part of the United Nations International Population Conference in Cairo, Egypt, in 1994, the Government of India decided to drop its focus on meeting targets for contraceptive use. It pledged, instead, to focus on the overall quality of life and empowerment of women and girls in areas such as reproductive health, nutrition, education, and economic empowerment. Women's groups argue that these measures will only succeed if there are concerted efforts to improve the status of women and girls within the family, and if males are also included in programs to take on more responsibility in promoting egalitarian family change. Evidence from several community-based organizations dealing with health, economic empowerment, and women's autonomy, reveals that when reproductive health issues are incorporated as an integral part of other efforts to improve the quality of life, women are in a better position to make decisions concerning the number of children. Most desire smaller families but lack information, power, and resources to fulfill their desire.

EDUCATION

As in most parts of the world, education is viewed as important in India to meet the needs of economic development, as well as improve the lives of individuals and families. However, social, cultural, and economic differences and inequalities of class, caste, and gender, as filtered through families, fundamentally shape educational achievements and the educational system.

Historically, formal education in India was limited to male Brahmans and, later, under Muslim rule, to higher-status males. Others received formal or informal instruction in the specialized trades and occupations. The British introduced the British educational system, mainly to develop skills necessary to assist in the administration of the colony. For the most part, it was mainly males from upper-status families who acquired the necessary education for administrative and new professional occupations. Formal education for higher-status girls also spread, and began to be seen as important if they were to fulfill their role as nurturers and caretakers of family needs. However, illiteracy was widespread

A girls band at the Lady Hawabai Jaffer Girls School founded for Muslim girls in Pune (Maharashtra) in the early 20th century. Photo Courtesy Lady Hawabai Jaffer Girls School.

at the time of independence. According to the 1951 census, the literacy rate was 16.1 percent, with male literacy at 27 percent and female literacy at 9 percent.

Trends since Independence

Motivated by the desire to develop India as a modern industrial and democratic society, the directive principles of the Indian Constitution stated that all Indians would be provided free and compulsory education through age 14 by 1960. Implementation of the directive, however, was left to each state, and the objective is yet to be achieved, even though in 1976 the Central Government assumed joint responsibility with the states to promote education. A new national policy on education was initiated in 1986 incorporating several proposals to improve access to education and the quality of education.

Although numerous improvements have been made, the goal of free and compulsory education for all has not yet been reached, and widespread inequities remain. According to the 1991 census, the literacy rate stood at 52.21 percent, with male literacy at 64.12 percent and female literacy at 39.29 percent. Although the rates are expected to be higher in the next census, current rates place India at about the same level as the average for Sub-Saharan Africa. Even there, countries such as Ghana, Tanzania, and Kenya have made tremendous improvements, and surpass India in literacy (Weiner 1991:161; Dreze and Sen 1995:30). And

India is still behind the literacy levels prevailing in many East Asian countries in the 1960s. South Korea, Thailand, and Hong Kong now have literacy rates of 90 to 100 percent, and China is at 80 percent (Dreze and Sen 1995:38–40). Although literacy rates in India have gone up, the actual number of illiterates has actually increased in India because of population growth.

Within India, there are significant variations in educational achievements. Literacy rate is nearly 90 percent in Kerala, and 38.5 percent in Bihar. In urban areas, the literacy rate is 73 percent, with 64 percent of females and 81 percent of males literate. In rural India, on the other hand, the literacy rate is only 44.69 percent, with male literacy at about 57 percent and female literacy at about 30 percent. People classified as Scheduled Castes (SCs) and Scheduled Tribes (STs) are disproportionately represented among the illiterate. Although constituting about 23 percent of the population, they accounted for more than one-third of the illiterate in the country according to the 1981 census. Among SCs male literacy was 37.7 percent and female literacy 13 percent, whereas among the STs 29.8 percent of the males and 9.6 percent of the females were literate. Separate figures from the 1991 census are not available, but literacy rates among these lower-status groups probably grew at a rate similar to the overall Indian population, about 8.6 percent (Shotton 1998:15–21)

The Structure and Functioning of Education

Early childhood education progresses to age 5. Primary school is from about ages 6 to 11 and covers class (or grade) 1 to class 5, followed by middle school until class 8, with secondary school (or high school) for classes 9 through 12, ending at about age 18. Institutions of higher education include technical schools providing two-year diplomas or degrees for up to five years of post-secondary education, as well as colleges and universities granting undergraduate and graduate degrees. At each level, institutions vary from being of high quality and well equipped, to those of poor quality and inadequate to almost nonexistent resources and facilities. Educational institutions are funded by the government for the most part, although there has been an increase in privately funded institutions, and those run by voluntary agencies.

Early childhood education is considered important to prepare children for formal schooling, to ensure appropriate development of children from the lower socioeconomic and disadvantaged groups, and to provide daycare for children of mothers in the paid labor force. Government programs have mainly targeted children of the poor. However, there are no uniform standards and regulations are not enforced. Many programs are no more than feeding centers while mothers work. There are now also some private institutions, some of high quality, in urban areas catering to the upwardly mobile middle classes. There has also been an increase in voluntary agencies such as the Self Employed Women's Association (SEWA) and Mobile Creche providing good quality preschool care to children of poor and working mothers. However, early childhood education is still extremely inadequate to meet the needs of all families and children (Swaminathan 1998).

Approximately 90 percent of children entering class I enroll in government schools, many of which lack facilities such as chalkboards, furniture, educational materials, and trained teachers. This is particularly true of schools in rural areas. Children from lower-status families tend to be enrolled in the worst schools. About 10 percent of the children, mostly from middle-class and wealthy families, attend private schools. Many of these also get some government funding. Included in this category are schools run by Christian churches and missionaries, and some of the elite schools. Many have a high level of academic rigor with the standard of education higher than at the same level in North American schools. They have tough entrance standards and are very competitive. Children are often burdened with homework and extra tutoring in order to succeed.

A key issue relates to enrollment, attendance, and dropout rates. A significant percentage of children of primary and secondary school age are not enrolled in schools. And even when they are enrolled, many do not attend school. The dropout rates are very high in the government schools that have poor facilities and standards, and dropout rates increase at higher grade levels. According to Government of India estimates, which are not always accurate, in 1988 about 99 percent of males and 83 percent of females at the primary school age level were enrolled in primary schools. At the secondary school level, however, only 41 percent of males and 29 percent of females in the relevant age group were enrolled. According to estimates of a 1985 study, of every 100 children enrolled in class 1, only 23 percent reached class 8. In the late 1980s, dropout rates in primary schools were much higher for females, SCs, and STs, at well over 50 percent, than for the general population, at 49 percent (Shotton 1998:21–26). Dropout rates are very low in the elite private schools.

In the last 20 to 30 years the curriculum has been standardized somewhat, and the National Council for Educational Research and Training (NCERT) has developed curriculum materials more suited to Indian, local, and regional conditions. School children sit for national examinations to graduate from class 10 and again from class 12. The failure rate, however, is very high, particularly in schools with inadequate facilities.

At the post-secondary level, by 1990–91 there were 177 universities, professional colleges for engineering, management, medicine, and agriculture; 500 teacher-training colleges; and a few thousand other colleges providing diplomas or undergraduate degrees. Although there has been a tremendous increase in enrollment in these institutions since independence, only about 5 percent of the population in the relevant age group are enrolled in post-secondary institutions, mostly males. The dropout rates are extremely high, at about 75 percent (Shotton 1998:21).

Graduates from some of the high-quality technical and professional schools are at the forefront of the small but growing number of high-tech and corporate enterprises in India. The southern Indian city of Bangalore, for example, has witnessed rapid growth in computer software development, and was recently named one of the top 10 "cybercities" in the world by *Newsweek* magazine. Graduates of elite schools in India are also disproportionately represented in graduate programs in computer science, engineering, mathematics, natural sciences, and management in North America. And in recent years, encouraged by economic liberalization, many have returned to India to set up high-tech and business enterprises.

Educational Inequalities and Deprivation

A variety of factors correlate to affect educational inequalities and deprivation. Partly because of the goals of modernization and economic development based on high-tech industries, the Indian government has spent a disproportionate amount of its education budget since independence on higher education. Many Indians take pride in asserting that India has the largest pool of scientists and engineers in the world. This fact, however, underscores the failures in primary and secondary education, and the elitist nature of educational access in India. In the early 1950s, about 55.6 percent of the total expenditure on education was allocated to elementary education. By the early 1990s this had declined to 25 percent. According to one study, in 1987 the expenditure per student per year was Rs 260.9 and Rs 301.4 for primary and secondary education. For higher education, the per capita expenditure was Rs 12,499 per year (at that time $1 U.S. was worth about Rs 15). And most students in institutions of higher education are from the upper and middle castes and classes. India also spends a lower percentage of its GDP on education than many other countries. The total expenditure on education has increased from 2.5 percent of the GDP in 1960 to 4.2 percent in 1989–90, but this is still lower than the 6 percent recommended if India is to make any significant progress (Shotton 1998:166–67).

Another factor associated with educational deprivation in India is the contribution of children to the household economy as paid and unpaid workers. According to estimates, about 8 to 10 percent of children are in the paid labor force. However, children under age 10 perform mainly household tasks and the number of hours worked is not enough to prevent schooling, although girls contribute significantly more to household tasks than boys. More children are in paid work at the middle and secondary school level. A more significant disincentive to schooling appears to be the direct costs of schooling. Although government schools do not charge tuition, the cost of books, stationery, clothes, extra tutoring, sports, and so on, are high for most poor families (Bhatty 1998:1731–36).

Poor quality of many schools associated with poor physical infrastructure, lack of curriculum materials, and shortage of dedicated teachers is a key factor affecting education. For example, only about half the schools have a properly constructed school building, about 42 percent of schools have only one classroom, only half have a suitable chalkboard, and more than half lack proper drinking water and toilets. Most schools have only one or two teachers, with only 15 percent of schools having more than four teachers. Teacher absenteeism is high and there is lack of accountability and a severe teacher shortage (Bhatty 1998:1736–39). These problems are most acute in government schools in rural areas.

Gender bias is a key factor contributing to educational inequality. There is widespread preference for male education because of perceived and real economic benefits for the family in a patrilocal and patrilineal family system. There is also concern over sending girls too far away from home for schooling. This bias against female education contradicts research that shows enormous benefits for the family as a result of female education, such as lower fertility, improved health and well-being, improved socioeconomic status, and empowerment. Several studies, however, do show considerable improvements in recent years (Bhatty 1998; Mukhopadhyay and Seymour 1994; Chanana 1988).

Current Efforts and Future Prospects

There is widespread recognition in India of the problems associated with education. The government as well as non-government agencies have initiated several programs. These include **nonformal education** programs for children and adults in poor and deprived groups and regions who for various reasons miss out on formal schooling. Many government programs have been implemented through cooperation with voluntary agencies; others are implemented by voluntary agencies receiving government funds or funds from national and international nonprofit agencies. Examples include the Total Literacy Campaigns in several districts, the Charvaha Vidyalaya in Turki, Bihar, PROPEL in Maharashtra, Eklavya in Madhya Pradesh, and Lok Jumbish in Rajasthan. There are also experimental schools, such as Mirambika in Delhi, Deepalaya also in Delhi, and the Bhubaneshwar School in Orissa.

Most effective are programs where the decision making is at the local level, staff is recruited and trained from the local communities, ideas and concerns of the local residents are incorporated into program development, there is focus on self-reliance and self-determination, and there is a nonhierarchical relationship between the teachers and learners. However, strong political will and sustained financial and moral commitment by the government are also crucial (Shotton 1998). Many argue that nonformal education alone will not be effective unless steps are taken to ban child labor and enforce compulsory education (Weiner 1991). They also note that the dominant upper and middle classes and castes have a deep-seated belief in the undesirability and inability of the lower-status groups to improve their status, in spite of rhetoric to the contrary. Changing this scenario will require enormous political will and an increase in expenditures and programs to reach everyone.

CONCLUSION

Many of the problematic as well as positive aspects of Indian society are filtered through the key social institutions of the family and education. The family is the site for gender and age differentiation and inequalities, but many see important benefits of strong and complex family ties. Also family roles and relationships vary by caste and class, and are undergoing significant changes. Changes in the family, however, are not unidirectional or homogeneous. Families and the individuals in them accommodate to their specific circumstances within the context of social and economic trends. Although gender, economic, and caste differences and inequalities are still perpetuated through the family and the educational system, there is considerable evidence of change and potential for change in the direction of greater equality and improvement in the quality of life. In spite of the unevenness of change, the situation is a dynamic one. And as we have seen in this and other chapters, the Indian state is a key player in the lives of Indians. In the next chapter, therefore, we will turn to a consideration of Indian politics and political processes.

CHAPTER 8

Political Institutions and Processes

Political leaders, scholars, and journalists often refer to India as "the world's largest democracy." A *New Yorker* article on the elections held in February–March 1998 starts with the comment "Half the people in the world who live in a democracy live in India. Yet India's recent general election was like nothing else on earth. For a start, there were more than six hundred million registered voters, and ballot boxes had to be transported by donkey, fishing boat, and mountain porter. There were nearly five thousand candidates, and some of these were unlikely parliamentarians" (French 1998: 36). The staggering number of registered voters accounts for much more than twice the total U.S. population, and upwards of 60 percent of these turned out to vote in India's 12th general elections since independence in 1947. India also has an elaborate system of democratic institutions at the national, state, and local levels.

When people refer to India as a democracy, however, they usually mean **liberal democracy.** The liberal interpretation of democracy, like the one prevalent in the United States, is associated with institutions of representative government, multiparty elections, separation of powers, individual freedom, and protection of various rights (Macpherson 1966: 35–45). Marxists, socialists, and other proponents of **participatory democracy,** however, argue that although liberal-democratic institutions provide a valuable framework for the exercise of individual rights, they do not ensure effective participation in the democratic process by people who are limited by factors such as class, gender, race, caste, and other cultural barriers. Participatory democracy, then, entails equal opportunities for all categories of people to participate in decisions affecting all arenas of human life including work, community, and interpersonal relations, in addition to formal political institutions. Effective participation can be built only upon egalitarian social and economic structures, and the process of democratization also entails, in this view, the creation of a just social order (Pateman 1970; Parry and Moran 1994). Politics, therefore, refers not just to the arena of formal political institutions associated with the state, and approved by the state, but also to activism in other aspects of people's lives.

Although India has in place all the ingredients of a liberal-democratic political system, the actual functioning of that system is fundamentally affected by a multitude of social, cultural, and economic inequalities and differences presented in earlier chapters. On the one hand, post-independence Indian politics is characterized by demands from various caste, religious, linguistic, and class groups, as well as women and the poor, for inclusion in the formal political process. On the other hand, we find numerous movements by these groups at the local community level for equality and social justice, and expansion of arenas for political and social action independent of the state.

In this chapter, I first describe the formal liberal-democratic political institutions established at the time of independence. How these institutions have functioned over the last half century is then analyzed in relation to social, cultural, and economic trends unique to India. Following this, I summarize some social movements that are an integral part of Indian politics. Finally, Indian political processes are placed within the global context.

FORMAL POLITICAL INSTITUTIONS

After a debate of over three years, the Constitution of India went into effect on January 26, 1950. A complex and lengthy document, it provides an institutional framework for governing the country, and a statement of philosophical goals, principles, and ideals to guide social policy. The key goals of the Constitution are to strengthen and protect national unity in a diverse and multicultural country, to create a democratic form of government and institutions, to promote social and economic equality through measures such as eradicating poverty, providing educational opportunities, ending unequal distribution of economic and other resources, abolishing caste and other forms of discrimination, and promoting religious freedom and tolerance. To preserve national unity, the Constitution confers special powers on the central government to limit rights, freedoms, and actions that are believed to undermine national territorial unity. However, within a federal structure, there is some autonomy for the states, and rights for religious, ethnic, and other cultural groups, although religion and ethnicity are not recognized as legitimate bases for electoral politics. The Constitution also proposes to promote national unity through the development of a national language, administrative system, and judicial system. In addition, there are numerous rights and freedoms, such as freedom of speech, movement, and association, right to private property, equality before the law, and protection against discrimination based on caste, sex, religion, place of birth and so forth (Austin 1993: 103–8).

As distinct from a presidential form of government such as that prevalent in the United States, India adopted a parliamentary system modeled on Great Britain. The official and ceremonial head of state is the president whose position is similar to the British monarch. The president has several executive powers, such as declaration of a state of emergency, suspension of fundamental rights in periods of crisis, and calling on the leader of the political party winning a majority of seats in elections to form a government. However, for the most part the president can exercise those rights only on the recommendation of the prime minister and the cabinet.

Like the United States and other Western liberal-democratic countries, in India too there is formal separation of powers between the executive branch, headed by the prime minister, the judiciary, headed by the Supreme Court, and the parliamentary legislature that is similar to the U.S. Congress. The prime minister is the head of government, and is usually the leader of the political party with a majority of seats in Parliament, or the party that is able to form an alliance with others in Parliament to gain majority support. This is different from the United States where the president is elected separately as the chief executive, and governs even when the political party to which the president belongs does not have a majority in Congress. The Indian Parliament has two houses, a lower house, the **Lok Sabha** or people's assembly, and an upper house, the **Rajya Sabha** or the council of states, loosely paralleling the U.S. House of Representatives and the Senate, respectively. Members of the Lok Sabha are elected from 542 constituencies all over India through universal adult suffrage with everyone over the age of 18 eligible to vote. The Lok Sabha member is elected for a five-year term, although elections can be called earlier if the party in power loses majority support. Of the 250 members in the Rajya Sabha, 238 are elected by the assemblies of the states within India, and 12 are nominated by the president on the basis of distinguished service to the country. The Supreme Court is headed by a chief justice and 25 associate justices, and there is a High Court in each state subordinate to it. The Supreme Court is charged with the protection of fundamental rights, judicial review, and resolving constitutional and policy disputes.

A similar political structure governs each of the 25 states within the Indian union. A governor is appointed by the president at the recommendation of the prime minister. However, the chief minister is the head of government, and there are two houses in the state legislature. Under India's federal system, the states have a certain degree of autonomy in conducting their affairs, although in practice the central government retains some key powers. The central government has control over defense, foreign affairs, energy, railways, interstate trade and commerce, and several duties and taxes. The state government is responsible for maintaining public order, local government, state public services, and agriculture. Economic and social planning and policy implementation, education, and criminal justice functions are the shared responsibility of the center and the states.

Cities, towns, districts (similar to counties), and villages are governed by a variety of self-governing institutions, but with very limited powers. At the time of independence, Gandhi, the leader of India's independence movement, argued that local councils or **Panchayats,** that predated British rule, should be revived and reformed as the basis for developing a decentralized and participatory democratic society, and that they should be at the forefront of rural social and economic development. Gandhi, however, died soon after independence, and the Western-oriented nationalist elite adopted the British parliamentary model with little effective devolution of power to local bodies. More recently, though, under a 1993 constitutional amendment on **Panchayati Raj** or rule of the local councils, more powers are to be transferred to the local councils, although the implementation so far has been uneven.

Assisting the central and state governments in administering the country and implementing policies is a large and complex bureaucracy. Three highly prestigious services at the all India level are the Indian Administrative Service, the Indian Foreign Service, and the Indian Police Service. Other branches of the central services are Revenue, Postal, Accounts and Audits, Railways, and Customs and Excise. There are also state-level services to deal with matters under their jurisdiction.

MAIN POLITICAL TRENDS SINCE INDEPENDENCE

Although the formal structure of political institutions in India has remained intact, in practice these institutions have been continuously challenged and modified. One key trend has been the struggle for power between the central government and the states, gradual erosion of the federal system, and pulls toward local and regional autonomy. While Jawaharlal Nehru as leader of the Indian National Congress, the party that led India to independence, was Prime Minister of India until 1964, the state governments had relative autonomy and there was little overt interference in their affairs. For the most part, however, the Congress was also in power in state assemblies. But the Congress came to be challenged in the states, and from within, after the death of Nehru. There was increasing unrest mainly due to economic crises and demands for political representation, and the central government assumed more powers. This happened particularly after Nehru's daughter, Indira Gandhi, became prime minister in 1966 and ruled for all but three years until 1984. There was more central intervention in state and local politics, decline of internal party organization and democracy, and more centralization of power within the Congress in the hands of Indira Gandhi and few close advisers. The low point came from 1975 to 1977 when, faced with mounting opposition, Indira Gandhi declared a state of emergency, suspended fundamental rights and took on dictatorial powers. After 1977, the Congress Party led by Indira Gandhi came to be termed Congress (I) or Indira Congress. The power of the Congress party, however, has considerably weakened since the late seventies. Regional political elites and parties have emerged to significantly affect state and national politics, and some parties, such as the Bharatiya Janata Party (BJP) or Indian people's party, have gained a larger national following (Brass 1994: 63–66).

This process, however, took place alongside increased mobilization of people from disadvantaged caste, economic, and social segments at the state and local levels for a greater share of economic resources, more effective political representation, and demands for regional, linguistic, and religious autonomy. Access to political power and influence on state policies are important because in India the state is responsible for both governing the country and managing and controlling economic resources. At the same time, however, the state has limited resources, and is unable to meet competing demands and expectations. And as various groups have mobilized to challenge the state and traditional forms of authority, leaders of other political parties, as in the Congress, have also tended to acquire more personal power and undermine internal party institutions. This has further reinforced the inability of the government and other state institutions to govern effectively and meet the needs of the people (Kohli 1990). These political trends can best be understood through the prism of electoral politics in India as they have unfolded in relation to various competing forces.

POLITICAL PARTIES AND ELECTORAL POLITICS

There are numerous political parties participating in elections in India. Some, such as the Congress, the Bharatiya Janata Party (BJP), the Janata Dal, the Communist Party of India (CPI), and the Communist Party of India (Marxist) (CPI-M), have varying degrees of support in more than one state. A significant development in post-independence India, however, is the emergence of numerous regional political parties in the states drawing support on the basis of one or more of the regional language, cultural, caste, and religious groups. The popularity and electoral success of most Indian political parties are connected to the personal qualities and strength of the party leader. Also there are many factions within the parties often based on caste, kinship, and religion, that become the basis of tensions and influence within the party and alliances with other parties for electoral gain (Baxter 1991: 102–19; Brass 1994: 67–94).

The Indian National Congress, founded in 1885, led India to independence, and in one form or another has led the Indian government for all but 8 of its first 52 years as an independent country. However, the domination of the Congress has declined since 1967. The Congress lost the national elections for the first time in 1977, came back to power in 1981, and lost again in 1989. It governed again from 1991 to 1996 with the support of some other parties, but failed to gain power in the 1996 and 1998 elections.

A key feature of the Congress has been the domination of members of the Nehru–Gandhi family as party leaders since independence. Nehru died in 1964, and after a brief stint as prime minister by Lal Bahadur Shastri, Indira Gandhi, who acquired the Gandhi name through marriage to someone not related to Mohandas Gandhi, became prime minister in 1966. Groomed into politics by her father, Indira Gandhi became very popular among the masses in her own right especially in the early 1970s. She groomed her younger son, Sanjay, as her political aid and leader of the Youth Congress. When Sanjay died in a plane crash in 1980, she persuaded her reluctant older son, Rajiv, to enter into politics. He was an airline pilot, married to an Italian woman, Sonia, who reportedly was vehemently opposed to Rajiv's becoming active in politics. When Indira Gandhi was assassinated in 1984, Rajiv, a political novice, became the prime minister. Rajiv himself was assassinated in 1991, by members of a Tamil militant group after which Narasimha Rao became the Congress leader and prime minister. After back-to-back defeats in the 1996 and 1998 elections, many Congressional supporters of the Nehru–Gandhi family urged Rajiv's influential widow, Sonia Gandhi, to emerge into public life and rescue the Congress from total disarray. She became Congress president in 1997, and plans to run for a seat in Parliament in the September–October 1999 elections. There is increasing speculation and controversy over the ironic possibility of an Italian-born naturalized citizen of India becoming India's prime minister should the Congress win the next elections.

Other Congress leaders have also been mainly from the elite and middle castes, particularly in northern India. However, the Congress has portrayed itself as a moderate party committed to democratic socialism and improving the lot of the disadvantaged groups, and as the only party capable of accommodating the needs of diverse groups in India. Until recently, it has managed to get the support from many among the lower social classes and castes and minority religions. However, the Congress, especially since the latter part of Indira Gandhi's rule, has also used religion and caste differences for political gain.

The BJP is a successor to the Jan Sangh, or people's association, that was founded in 1951. Although claiming to be representative of all Indians, the Jan Sangh drew most of its support from rural and urban Hindu elite and middle castes and classes, and mostly in northern and central India. Reconstituted as the BJP in the late 1970s, it has emerged as the political leader of Hindu nationalism in India arguing for a strong and united India based on the Hindu way of life, although it claims to define Hinduism as an inclusive and tolerant religion. The BJP has made significant electoral gains in the last decade, and after the February–March 1998 elections it formed the Indian government with the support of several regional political parties. However, to gain electoral support and power, the moderate wing of the BJP has displayed pragmatism, underplayed Hindu nationalism, and tried to present itself as a secular political party representing all Indians and committed to socioeconomic development. However, conservative Hindu nationalist groups as well as factions within the BJP have been emboldened by the electoral power of the BJP into pushing their agendas, and harassing and attacking members of minority religions. And in April 1999, the BJP lost majority support in Parliament, and India is headed for elections yet again.

India's two main communist parties, the CPI and CPI (M), derive ideological inspiration from the Soviet and Chinese communist parties, respectively. However, in India, they have gradually become more reformist rather than revolutionary and participate in electoral politics in search of political power. They are strongest in West Bengal and to some extent in Kerala.

A variety of noncommunist parties opposing the Congress (I) and the BJP, representing mainly middle agricultural castes and peasants, small entrepreneurs and industrialists, and some regional groups, formed a coalition that defeated the Congress (I) in 1977, but the coalition fell apart in 1979. Some remnants formed the Janata Dal, and led the Indian government from 1989 until late 1990. And again, in 1996 until late 1997, some of these groups became part of the United Front coalition governing India. However, ridden with conflicts, none of the coalition governments lasted anywhere near their five-year term of office.

As already noted, many regional political parties, such as the Dravida Munnetra Kazhagam (DMK) in Tamil Nadu, Akali Dal in Punjab, the Asom Gana Parishad (AGP) in Assam, and the Shiv Sena in Maharashtra, have gained support in their respective states. For the most part they have demanded more state and regional autonomy. From time to time, as in the 1998 parliamentary elections, the Congress, BJP, and United Front have formed alliances with the regional parties. As a result, many members from the regional parties have become members of the Indian Parliament, and play a crucial role in determining the fate of the Indian government.

Results of the last four general elections held in India in 1989, 1991, 1996, and 1998 indicate that no single political party is able to get the majority of seats in Parliament, and India has entered a stage of coalition government. Many view this diversification of political support as a reflection of the fragmentation and instability of Indian society and politics. Others, however, view this trend as a reflection of India's unique cultural, linguistic, and religious diversity, and the incorporation of this diversity into the democratic political process as an indicator of the resilience of Indian democracy. Recent public opinion polls of registered voters show a significant faith in the electoral and democratic process, even though many are concerned over corruption, unemployment, inflation, national unity, law and order, and so on, and are skeptical of the ability of politicians to govern well (*India Today*, August 31, 1996:28–43; *India Today*, August 18, 1997:24–35). These polls also show that there has been a gradual increase in voter turnout from about 45 percent in 1952 to about 60 to 65 percent now. The increase is largely due to greater participation by middle and lower castes and classes, peasants, and women. These groups also show more faith in electoral politics.

Caste plays an important role in Indian politics. The Indian Constitution provides for the reservation of certain electoral districts for candidates from the lower castes and tribes. Some caste-based political parties have been formed to participate in elections, such as the Republican Party of India formed by B. R. Ambedkar, a leader of the Dalits in western India, in the 1950s, and more recently the Bahujan Samaj Party (BSP) representing Dalits in northern India. In rural areas in particular people are more likely to vote for a candidate from their own caste, and if a particular caste tends to be dominant in a particular area, political parties may be prompted to put up a candidate from that caste for election.

In recent years, there is a definite increase and diversification in the number and nature of groups seeking to influence elections and policies. These include trade unions, business groups, peasants and farmers, students, intellectuals, religious groups, and women's groups. Moreover, as noted in Chapter 6, a constitutional amendment in 1993 instituted the reservation of 33 percent of seats in local village and town councils for women, and there is now a debate over the issue of reservation of the same percentage of seats for women in state-level and parliamentary elections.

POLITICS OF LANGUAGE, REGION, AND RELIGION

Claims for regional autonomy in relation to one or more of language, religion, and ethnic identity have posed the most significant challenges to the unity of the Indian national state, and have undermined India's claims to be democratic. These claims are not unique to India, as recent events such as the breakup of the Soviet Union, the breakup of Yugoslavia, and examples of Canada, Ireland, Belgium, the Middle East, and several other countries illustrate.

To comprehend these processes, it is useful to define and distinguish between the notions of nation and state. A **nation** may be defined as a group of people who share, or believe that they share, a common culture, sense of belonging, and varying degrees of political consciousness on the basis of one or more of language, religion, ancestry, and other shared experiences often in relation to a territorial region over which they may or may not have political control. A sense of national identity, however, does not automatically exist among people sharing a common language or religion, but is created and also changed through cultural and political actions.

A **state** (as distinct from states within a country such as the United States) is a territorial unit usually recognized as politically independent with sovereignty in governing and administering its affairs. A state is in effect a synonym for a country, and there are several institutions related to the state that enable governance. Leaders of most states desire to unify the population as a nation with a common bond, even though in many instances they may have multi-ethnic populations that may claim separate political identity as a nation. A common desire of nations is to have a state corresponding with its nationality and hence claim to be a **nation-state** or to have some autonomy in relation to the state. **Nationalism,** then, is a movement to create a nation-state, or attain some degree of political autonomy, or even to create a sense of national identity.

Indian leaders, therefore, claim that India is a nation-state sharing a common historical culture that accommodates linguistic, religious, and cultural diversity. Many of these groups, however, challenge that claim and have demanded more autonomy and/or outright independence. These processes must be understood within the context of the inability of state institutions to meet the economic and social needs of the people, the weakening of the Congress and the concentration of power in personal hands, and the manipulation of religion, language, caste, and community ties for political power. I will illustrate these through a discussion of language politics, as well as the cases of Punjab, Kashmir, and Assam and the Northeast that have been significant in recent years.

Language and Politics

As noted in Chapter 2, India exhibits enormous linguistic diversity. The exact number of people speaking, reading and writing, or understanding a particular language is unknown. However, Hindi is the largest single language spoken. One estimate in 1995 puts the number of Hindi speakers at 43 percent of the population (Heitzman & Worden 1996: 182). A recent nationwide survey states that 66 percent of Indians speak Hindi, whereas a little less than 50 percent can read and write Hindi, and 71 percent claim to understand Hindi (*India Today*, August 18, 1997:31). About

94 percent of North Indians speak or understand Hindi, but only about a quarter of South Indians do. A significant proportion of the population speaks more than one language, however, and Hindi may not be the native language of all who speak or understand it. Approximately 5 percent or less speak each of the other languages. English is also an important language spoken all over India, particularly among the elite. It is now taught in over 50 percent of schools. But according to the nationwide survey mentioned above, about 19 percent speak English, and about a third read, write, and understand it, again mostly in the urban areas.

As part of the constitutional guarantee to recognize and accommodate the interests of each language group, the Indian government promised to reorganize the boundaries of states in India so that most speakers of a particular language had their own separate state. This was meant to allow the development of the local language, and the intent was that all official business within the state would be in that language. However, Hindi was to be phased in as the national language and the language of official business between the central government and the states by 1965 as a means of promoting national unity. Until then, English was to be used as the language "linking" the different parts of the country. By the late 1970s most language groups had their separate states. Linguistic reorganization was most successful in areas where speakers of a particular language were concentrated in a particular territorial area, and where dominant groups were able to mobilize the popular support for the cause. But when the time came to institute Hindi as the official language, political parties and groups in the non-Hindi speaking states mobilized to protest the imposition of Hindi. Under a compromise in 1967, English was recognized as an additional official language for use by the states in addition to their native language. However, in many of the reorganized states, there are many linguistic minorities whose native tongues are not officially recognized. Although these minority languages are supposed to be protected, in most instances, the dominant state language has become stronger at the expense of the minority languages (Brass 1994: 157–74).

The potential for conflict is greatest where language politics and Central Government policies interact with issues such as religious and tribal identities, and regional socioeconomic and political issues, as in Punjab, Assam and the Northeast, and Jammu and Kashmir (Kashmir). An added dimension in Punjab, Assam and the Northeast, and Kashmir has been the concentration of the minority ethnic and/or religious group in a unified territorial space.

Punjab

At the time of independence, the state of Punjab also included the present-day states of Haryana and Himachal Pradesh. The state included Hindi and Punjabi speakers, and was home to a majority of the people adhering to the Sikh religion. As part of the movement for reorganization of states on the basis of language, Punjab was divided into three states by 1966. A smaller state of Punjab emerged with a slight majority of Sikhs in the population. A moderate political party, the Akali Dal, deriving most of its support from the rural Sikh agricultural classes, came to power after the 1967 state elections. They demanded resolution of some outstanding issues not dealt with at the time of the reorganization of the state. These included transfer of the capital of the united Punjab, Chandigarh, to the new state of Punjab, the allocation of water from two rivers, Ravi and Beas, between Punjab and Haryana, and settling a territorial dispute over a region being claimed by both Punjab and Haryana.

In an attempt to destabilize the Akali Dal government and create divisions among the Sikhs, the Indian government, led by Indira Gandhi, encouraged some militant Sikh groups to mobilize against the moderate Akalis on the pretext that the Akalis were not representing Sikh interests. The move backfired, leading to an increase in power of the militants, and an escalation during the 1980s of a movement for the creation of an independent Sikh state called Khalistan. The movement was met with increased police and military repression, and suspension of democratic politics, leading to the alienation of most Sikhs from the Central Government that was interpreted as representing Hindu interests.

A key event was the military attack ordered by the then prime minister, Indira Gandhi, on the Golden Temple in Amritsar, the holiest Sikh shrine, on June 5, 1984. Religious sites are usually exempt from police and military intervention. But Indira Gandhi justified the attack because the militant leader, Jarnail Singh Bhindranwale, and his supporters had taken refuge in the Golden Temple complex, and over the course of several months had fortified and armed themselves. The complex was destroyed and hundreds killed, hurting deeply even the majority of Sikhs who did not support the militants. Ironically, because of British colonial policies, Sikhs continue to be disproportionately represented in the Indian army, and have served loyally, forming about 30 percent of the commissioned officers. Many Sikhs were in regiments participating in the attack on the Golden Temple and military operations in other parts of the Punjab. This move caused deep disaffection, creating a context within which Indira Gandhi was assassinated by two of her Sikh bodyguards on October 31, 1984. This event was marked by large-scale violence and killing of over 3,000 Sikhs in the Indian capital, Delhi, and other parts of northern India. The carnage was orchestrated by local Congress leaders who have not yet been punished in spite of efforts by civil rights groups.

Indira Gandhi's son, Rajiv, as prime minister, initially tried to resolve the Punjab issue through a treaty with moderate Sikh leaders, but the accord was not implemented. The conflict continued, and the militant

movement was eventually crushed in 1992. The militants also lost support because they too started engaging in increased extortion, rape, and
torture of a Punjab population tired of so many years of strife (Brass
1994: 193–201). Many of the outstanding issues, however, remain unre-
solved even though there has been a return of an elected government,
and in the most recent elections in 1997 a moderate wing of the Akali Dal
party returned to power.

Interestingly, Punjab is agriculturally the most productive state in
India with a higher-than-average growth rate and low poverty. However, capital-intensive agricultural development created a section of very
rich farmers, while marginalizing other farmers. There was increased
debt and low return on investment. Moreover, agricultural growth was
not matched by corresponding growth in opportunities for the mostly
Sikh rural population in industry, trade, and business that continued to
remain concentrated in the hands of the Hindus. As noted in the chapter
on the economy, the problem of unemployment and underemployment
has grown all over India. But in Punjab this issue was complicated by political manipulation of religious identities. Many frustrated and disgrun-
tled youth, in particular, went on to support militant Sikh nationalism, a
move reinforced by state repression (Narang 1988).

The Northeast and Assam

The Northeast region of India, a mostly hilly region surrounding the
Brahmaputra River valley and its tributaries, was once called the North
East Frontier Agency and later Assam. At the time of independence, the
region included native Assamese speakers, most of whom were Hindus;
Bengali speakers, mostly Hindus and some Muslims, most of whom migrated during the British period; many hill and plains tribal groups,
many of them converted to Christianity by missionaries. As a result of
movements for reorganization of states in the 1950s and 1960s, most of
the regions populated by the main tribal groups were granted statehood,
leading to the formation of Nagaland, Meghalaya, Arunachal Pradesh,
and Mizoram. Although they gained limited autonomy, significant
groups in these states as well as in Manipur, Tripura, and Assam want
complete independence from India. The Indian army and security forces
maintain a strong presence in these areas to suppress these demands,
even though there is considerable amount of unrest and instability
(Weiner 1978; Dasgupta 1998; Brass 1994: 201–15).

The formation of the tribal states highlighted the economic and linguistic differences between the native Assamese speakers and the Bengali Hindu migrants. The latter, encouraged to migrate by the British to
assist in administering and economically developing the region, came to
dominate the middle-class administrative and professional positions.

Although Assam is India's biggest oil producer and the center of production for one of India's leading exports, tea, most of these industries are controlled by non-Assamese. Bengali was also the medium of instruction in schools until the Assamese gained a majority in the state legislature. They then moved to make Assamese the state language although the Bengalis want a dual-language policy. The newly emerging Assamese middle classes, however, find opportunities limited as a result of outside control of institutions.

There was large-scale illegal immigration of Bengali Muslims and Hindus from Bangladesh in the 1970s. And it was mainly over the issue of expulsion of illegal immigrants that the All Assam Students Union (AASU) launched an agitation in 1979 that turned increasingly militant and separatist. The Indian government signed a peace accord in 1985 to deal with migration and economic development, and an Assamese political party growing out of the AASU, the Asom Gana Parishad (AGP) came to power in the state assembly. The AGP government, however, failed to live up to its promises and the accord was not fully implemented. This gave rise to the campaign by the United Liberation Front of Assam (ULFA), formed in 1980, for complete separation from India. Support for the ULFA comes mainly from the educated and unemployed Assamese youth, and the main targets are government officials, bureaucrats, and owners of industry and business. A tenuous situation continues in spite of a strong military presence and some offers of economic development proposals. Meanwhile, the Bodo tribes in Assam have launched a movement for autonomy, and even though the Bodo Autonomous Council was formed in 1993, the movement has not fully subsided.

Kashmir

The northernmost Indian states of Jammu and Kashmir present another dimension of regional politics that challenges the unity and legitimacy of national state boundaries in India (Widmalm 1998; Navlakha 1996; Talbot 1991). Kashmir is the only state in India that has a Muslim majority, and as such Pakistan has staked claim to it as part of Pakistan. Three wars over Kashmir have been fought between India and Pakistan. However, a significant percentage of the population in the Ladakh region bordering China are Buddhist and Tibetan, and in other parts, particularly in the southwest region of Jammu, they are Hindus, mainly Dogras and Brahmans. At the time of India's independence the region was ruled by Hindu Dogra Kings, and Brahmans, known as Kashmiri Pandits, were in higher-status administrative and professional positions. The Kashmiri Muslims were mainly artisans, peasants, and service workers until the mid-20th century. When India and Pakistan were partitioned in 1947, the ruler initially decided to remain independent, but turned to India for help when Pakistan invaded in 1948 and occupied about 40 percent of the territory. Although a United Nations resolution proposed a referendum to decide over the control of Kashmir, both the Indian and Pakistani governments continue to lay claim to the entire region. As a way to keep Kashmir within India, the Indian Constitution under Article 370 grants special status to Kashmir granting it autonomy to run its own affairs and institute its own laws in all areas except defense, foreign affairs, and communications.

In the last 50 years, however, there has been no satisfactory policy in relation to Kashmir. Many Kashmiris, and activists and intellectuals outside Kashmir, argue that the Government of India has consistently undermined Kashmiri autonomy by frequently interfering in local state politics. It has also continued to promote Hindu interests, they argue, even though Indian government assistance has resulted in some economic development and modernization. However, many conservative groups within India, such as the right-wing Hindu organizations and the BJP, argue that Kashmir is an integral part of India and should not have special status.

Since the 1970s, the Congress government in India has interfered more in state politics, and has entered into an alliance with the National Conference party in Kashmir. When the National Conference-Congress alliance won the 1987 state elections, the opposition alleged widespread rigging of elections and launched an increasingly volatile militant movement. Whereas some militants want union with Pakistan, the Jammu and Kashmir Liberation Front (JKLF) and several other groups want a separate country. As Pakistan continues to support and train the militants, the Indian military and paramilitary forces are engaged in a protracted battle resulting in repression and human rights violations leading to widespread alienation of the general Kashmiri Muslim population. Much of the Hindu population in the worst affected areas have fled. Fresh elections were held in the state in September 1996 in which the National Conference came to power, but the elections were boycotted by groups wanting independence. As the government tries to bring about some stability amid signs that the population is lessening support for militants, the Indian army continues to maintain a strong presence in the wake of continuing militancy in many parts of the state. No Indian government, however, has been able to come up with a long-term solution. Many activists, intellectuals, and leaders see hope only in according true autonomy to the state and assistance in rebuilding the economy.

Overview

These three cases highlight the competing interpretations of nationalism in India discussed in detail in Chapter 3. The Congress officially claims that India is a secular nation inclusive of all religious and cultural groups and provides protection for all minorities. However, Congress politics since independence have been interpreted by minority religions as promoting India as a Hindu nation, while also manipulating religion and caste for electoral gains. This has led to a perception among non-Hindus that they are being forced to assimilate. Many middle-and upper-caste Hindus, however, believe that too many concessions are being given to minorities thereby undermining the strength and unity of India. These issues become volatile when linked to economic grievances and manipulation of state politics for electoral gain. It is important to note that movements and conflicts related to region, religion, language, and caste in India are not due to "deep-seated" and "ancient" antagonisms. Discourses of religious, caste, linguistic, and regional identities have, instead, been constructed within the context of the manipulation of these forms of cultural identities for political power and influence by central government and local political elites (see e.g., Bose and Jalal 1997; Basu and Kohli 1998).

Moreover, regional movements, either for secession from India or for the reorganization of state boundaries within India are in effect calls for more regional and local autonomy, self-government, and participatory democracy. They are critiques of the inability of formal liberal-democratic political institutions and electoral politics to be truly representative and inclusive. In the last decade, however, there have been some moves toward greater local self-government and regional autonomy as long as the demand is not for secession from India. Recently, a consensus seems to be emerging on creating separate states of Jharkhand, a hilly region populated mainly by tribal groups in east-central India incorporating parts of the states of Bihar, Madhya Pradesh, Bengal and Orissa, Uttarkhand, a mostly mountainous part of northern Uttar Pradesh, and the Chattisgarh region in Madhya Pradesh. All these regions are rich in natural resources but a large proportion of the assets is controlled by outsiders, whereas the native population remains largely disadvantaged socially and economically and does not benefit from economic and industrial development.

It should be noted, though, that India's liberal-democratic political structure affords opportunities for political mobilization of people as well as accommodation of competing demands. However, liberal-democratic institutions have been in operation in India for a much shorter time than, for instance, in the United States. Whereas the United States became independent in 1776, India only achieved independence in 1947. The United States did not extend voting rights to women until 1920, and full legal civil rights were not extended to African Americans until the 1960s. Indeed, nearly nine decades after independence, the United States was embroiled in a civil war that threatened its unity, and nonwhite immigrants were restricted from becoming U.S. citizens until

1952. In other words, in spite of a very liberal and democratic Constitution drawn up soon after independence, the United States has struggled to put its various provisions into practice. Is it perhaps too much to expect a diverse and complex country such as India to have a smooth ride on the path to democratization over a much shorter period of time?

GRASSROOTS MOVEMENTS, CIVIL SOCIETY, AND THE STATE

Many of India's movements for autonomy are the result of mobilization of people at the grassroots, in the sense that they derive their support from the people in the local communities, and represent or claim to represent community interests. Historically also, there is evidence of community-based participation in voluntary groups, resistance to authority, and movements for local control and social reform in India. However, there were relatively few movements against the Indian state in the first two decades after independence. The communist-led poor peasant movement in Telangana in the southern Indian state of Andhra Pradesh was crushed in the late 1940s. But in the late 1960s and early 1970s, the communist-inspired naxalbari movement, based in the Naxalbari region in West Bengal, challenged the power of the big landlords. Indian communist parties also mobilized peasants and workers in some other parts of India.

In the last three decades, however, there has been an enormous increase in grassroots organizations and other non-government voluntary groups that are independent of state and electoral politics. They are an integral part of social movements and actions among groups such as lower castes, the poor, peasants, landless agricultural laborers, tribal groups, and women fighting for equality and social justice and focusing on a variety of economic, cultural, and environmental issues. These movements have become an important part of the Indian political landscape, and are movements for a more participatory democracy in India. If we define **social movements** as organized efforts to bring about some form of social change or to resist change, then social movements are also, by definition, political movements.

A variety of social and political processes have precipitated these movements. A key factor has been the failure of state-orchestrated economic development policies to eradicate poverty and improve the quality of life of the large proportion of the population as discussed in Chapter 5. In fact, the benefits of uneven capitalist economic development and liberal-democratic politics have mainly benefited the middle and upper castes and classes, and some sections of the poor, and lower castes, leading to large-scale marginalization (Omvedt 1993; Shiva 1989; Kothari 1989, 1990).

At the same time, the rhetoric of democracy and establishment of democratic political institutions and electoral politics have led to large-scale mobilization of people to demand their rights. Nonparty grassroots social action groups and other non-government voluntary organizations have emerged in rural and urban areas to challenge the parliamentary model of liberal democracy, and the dominant state model of socioeconomic development. They have emerged as an important part of the process to broaden the concept of democracy, create and expand alternative spaces for social and political action, and redefine the form and content of legitimate politics as conventionally perceived (Kothari 1989; Tandon 1991; Pandey 1991).

These social movement organizations relate to the state in a variety of ways. Most are critical of state policies and work to change them. Some do so in a confrontational manner; others attempt to engage state officials through cooperative efforts, depending on local circumstances and the ideological philosophy underlying their work. Many groups work at the community level to enhance awareness and understanding of issues as part of action to change conditions. These local efforts are often complemented by forming networks with other organizations on particular issues to influence local, state and, national government officials and agencies. Government agencies and officials are sometimes responsive and supportive, and sometimes not. They are willing to allow local self-help efforts so long as these are not interpreted as being too "disruptive" to the state.

In many of these organizations, such as the Community Rural Health Project, Action India, the Self Employed Women's Association described in the chapter on gender relations, middle-class and educated youth, intellectuals, and professionals have emerged as active participants and catalysts for change. Equipped with knowledge about larger economic, legal, and social currents and skills in dealing with officials and bureaucrats, they share this knowledge with the disadvantaged groups. More important, however, many middle-class activists have made an effort to learn from the disadvantaged sections, have developed a partnership with them, and have worked with the disadvantaged groups to enable them to articulate their needs and develop programs in terms that they can define and manage. Other middle-class activists have formed research and documentation centers on a range of social, political, cultural, economic, and environmental issues, such as the Centre for Women's Development Studies in New Delhi, Aalochana Centre for Documentation and Research on Women, in Pune in Maharashtra State, Centre for Science and the Environment, and Participatory Research in Asia both in New Delhi. As such, they initiate and influence debates on these issues and seek to influence state policy and grassroots social action.

Several groups of poor and middle peasants, landless agricultural laborers, tribal groups, forest dwellers and fish workers, and women, for example, have organized over issues such as wages and working conditions, debt and bonded labor, exploitation by upper castes and larger landowners, gender inequality and patriarchal institutions, health, education, economic empowerment, loss of control over their lands, and displacement because of various economic development projects. Mechanization of agriculture, for instance, has benefited a few while leading to unemployment and underemployment for others. The same process has destabilized fishing communities with mechanized trawlers gaining control and also resulting in depletion of fish stock. Forest dwellers are displaced and threatened by factors such as logging and deforestation, government policies that limit local access to the forests, the building of large dams, mining operations, and industrial projects. In many cases the powerlessness of these groups is connected to lower caste, tribal, and gender status (Shah 1988; Omvedt 1993). Since the mid-1980s, in particular, women have emerged as important participants in the peasant, workers, tribal, and environmental movements. They have sought to make their voices heard and create spaces within these movements (Omvedt 1993:199–231; Sen 1990).

Interestingly, though, activists in these new social movements are not necessarily against modern technological and commercial developments. For example, the farmers' movements of the 1970s and 1980s derive their support from small and independent commercial farmers fighting for easier access to credit and inputs, such as fertilizers, irrigation, electricity, fair prices for crops, and freedom from debt. They are against state control of economic development and the power of larger agribusiness companies and market forces that cannot be locally controlled. In fact the farmers' movements have been most active in the more commercialized areas of the country such as parts of Maharashtra, Karnataka, Punjab, Haryana, and western Uttar Pradesh. Also, in many instances, the farmers, many from the lower castes, have also incorporated the agricultural laborers' demands for fair wages as part of their struggles, even as the mobilization of landless agricultural laborers by the communist parties has declined (Omvedt 1993:100–26).

Many of these movements have had significant local, state, national, and even international impact. Whereas movements among the lower castes or Dalits are discussed in Chapter 4, and women's movements are discussed in Chapter 6, I will here discuss environmental activism in India. Initially, ecological concerns formed the basis of many of the movements among the rural poor. Increasingly, environmental movements in India have highlighted the destruction of the environment and local culture and lifestyles in the name of economic development. Local activists have networked with other non-government organizations and the media to highlight the distinction between destructive development and **sustainable development** that would keep the needs of local people and the environment as the central focus of development.

One significant movement is the Chipko movement that started in 1972 in the hill areas of Uttarkhand in the northwestern part of Uttar Pradesh and takes its name from its tactic of non-violent resistance to tree-felling by mass hugging of trees by the local people. In addition to generating national and international attention, there was debate among different wings within the movement over appropriate ways to resist environmental degradation and promote economic development to meet the needs of the local people and involve them in the decision-making process. Women became very active in the movement and were much more concerned with protecting forests for fuel and fodder than the men who were often more willing to allow commercial felling of trees (Sharma 1987; Berreman 1989). Two of the leaders of the movement, Vimla and Sundarlal Bahuguna, are now actively resisting the building of the Tehri Dam in the region that many environmental experts believe is ecologically fragile.

A sustained struggle has taken place since the mid-1980s in the Narmada River Valley in Maharashtra, and parts of Madhya Pradesh and Gujarat, over the proposal to build numerous dams for power generation and irrigation (Kothari 1991). The movement against the project developed over the issues of environmental destruction, high cost, displacement of people because of widespread submergence of land, and the benefits going mainly to people in urban areas and in Gujarat state. Support for the movement came from numerous grassroots organizations, environmentalists, economists, irrigation experts and intellectuals, and several international environmental organizations, with the Narmada Bachao Andolan, or "struggle to save the Narmada," led by Medha Patkar, being the most active. Eventually, the World Bank withdrew financial support for the project following an independent study. But even before that the Indian government decided to go ahead with the project without World Bank funding, and launched a counter movement to support it. Within the movement, the focus has now shifted toward limiting the size of the dams, building smaller dams and tanks to limit destruction and displacement, and ensuring appropriate rehabilitation of people who are being uprooted from their homes as a result of the project. Leaders of this movement, and other environmental organizations, are increasingly forming alliances with one another in order to influence state policies, and increase the participation of local people in the management of environmental resources.

The struggle over the Narmada River dams emerged within the context of the debate over alternatives to state-orchestrated development projects. In the people's science movement, for example, modern Western science is criticized as being colonial and destructive. Whereas some wings of the movement tend to idealize the "traditional" culture as they conceive it, many activists have developed plans and designs for alternative and small-scale technologies that use low levels of energy, and can be locally managed and controlled. These movements are not against technology and modernity per se. And although putting many of these plans into practice has so far been sporadic, the vocabulary of alternative development has emerged as a challenge for the Indian state.

Grassroots and other nongovernment organizations have, therefore, emerged as an important part of the democratic process in India. They are often too focused on their specific tasks and issues and do not form consistent alliances, but these linkages are beginning to grow. Not all groups are well organized or democratic in their functioning. But collectively they have had an impact on government rhetoric and policies, although implementation of policies remains problematic.

INDIA IN THE GLOBAL CONTEXT

India's internal political policies, debates, and processes are also shaped by its position in the global system of states. Soon to be the most populated country in the world, India occupies an important place in the world. India's global position is characterized by a dynamic tension between its desire to be politically, economically, and militarily strong and independent in the region and the world, and a desire by other countries to contain India's power while opening up its markets and economy to global capitalism (Bouton 1987; Cohen 1991).

Contact with European traders and colonial rule drew the Indian subcontinent into part of the world political–economic system. As its largest colony, Britain developed parts of India that produced goods and provided raw materials for the development of British industry, while India was used as a market for British goods. In the post-independence period, Indian leaders stressed the need to be economically and politically self-reliant and strong. Economically, this entailed protecting and developing Indian industry, agriculture, and markets while limiting foreign capital to perceived interests of the country. Politically, this meant a focus on India's internal and regional security, limiting third-country intervention in resolving disputes with neighboring countries, maintaining self-reliance and independence by adopting a policy of "nonalignment" in international affairs, and emerging as a leader in regional and world affairs.

A key issue in the region has been India's problematic relation with Pakistan, particularly over the Kashmir issue. Although both India and Pakistan claim sovereignty over Kashmir, Pakistan has also been concerned with India's size and military strength. As a result, Pakistan has sought alliances with the United States, China, and its Islamic neighbors to the west. Initially, India tried to contain China by befriending it, but then fought a war with the much more powerful China in 1962, a war that was disastrous for India. Thereafter, India developed stronger economic and military ties with the former Soviet Union, even as Pakistan developed ties with China and the United States. Officially, though, India became a leader of the "Non-Aligned Movement," composed mostly of several less-industrialized countries of Asia, Africa, and Latin America that determined to remain independent of both United States and Soviet influence during the Cold War years. In practice, though, India has chosen its position on issues based on what it considered to be in its best strategic interest at the time. India has not fought an official war with Pakistan since 1971 when India assisted Bengali Muslims in East Pakistan to break away and form Bangladesh. However, tensions have escalated over the issue of Pakistan's covert assistance for militants in Punjab and Kashmir in 1980s and 1990s. Another controversial issue is the development of nuclear weapons in the region. India tested its first nuclear device in 1974, and then conducted another round of tests in May 1998 citing threats from China and China's longterm assistance to Pakistan in developing Pakistan's nuclear capability. Pakistan retaliated in late May with its own nuclear tests. In early 1999 there were some moves to improve relations between the two countries. But the optimistic mood was shattered in May 1999 by the discovery by the Indian army of numerous military posts inside the Indian-held part of Kashmir by Pakistani-backed armed fighters and Pakistani army personnel, leading to intensive military warfare.

India's relations with the United States are connected with the United States' relations with China, Pakistan, and earlier, the Soviet Union. As U.S. relations with China thawed and the Cold War with the Soviet Union continued, the United States became the biggest arms supplier and aid-giver to Pakistan. This assistance to Pakistan grew during the 1980s when the Soviet Union occupied Afghanistan, and the United States assisted the Afghan resistance based in Pakistan. However, U.S. military assistance to Pakistan declined after the withdrawal of the Soviet Union in the early 1990s. Since then the United States has attempted to contain both India and Pakistan. Indo–U.S. relations remain strained over the issue of defense and nuclear weapons. India refuses to sign the Nuclear Non-Proliferation Treaty, accusing the five original nuclear power states of not destroying their own vast supplies of nuclear weapons. Economically, however, the United States has emerged as India's largest trading partner, especially after the fall of the Soviet Union and economic liberalization policies adopted by India since the early 1990s.

In the last two decades, however, India has also sought to expand its economic ties with other countries in East Asia, the Middle East, Europe, and the successor states of the Soviet Union. Despite some tensions, particularly with Sri Lanka during the 1980s and early 1990s, India's relations with other neighboring countries, Nepal, Bangladesh, and Bhutan, remain peaceful and mostly friendly.

CONCLUSION

It is clear that Indian politics exhibits a diversity matching its economic, social, and cultural diversity. The Indian Constitution is at the center of debates representing different viewpoints and different sections of society. These debates focus on interpretations of the Constitution, state policies, institutions of parliamentary democracy, nature of technological and economic change, and issues of social justice and equality. These debates take place not just within electoral politics and formal political institutions, but also through a range of movements and actions by different groups. The sheer variety and range of these political processes and movements cause many observers to despair over India's future as a democracy. The frequent elections and failed coalitions as well as numerous alliances and competing demands from numerous categories of people have led some to argue that India is almost impossible to govern (see e.g., Kohli 1990). Indeed, the Indian political scene is very often chaotic. Many other observers, however, see in these debates and processes an indication of the strength and depth of democratic values and institutions in India (e.g., Kothari 1993). Struggles for freedom and democracy do cause tension and uncertainty, but also hold out hope for a more democratic future even in the face of opposing forces, they argue. Indians also proudly point out that India is "the world's largest democracy." However, they are also aware that Indian democracy is profoundly undermined by its key failures in the economic sphere, particularly its failure to eradicate poverty, and various instances of violence against women, minorities, and the poor.

CHAPTER 9

Social Change in India

When I was an undergraduate student in New Delhi, the capital of India, in the mid-1970s, there was a billboard advertising "Amul butter" on one of the main streets from central Delhi to the South Delhi area where my college was located. This brand of butter was manufactured by a state-owned enterprise connected to the National Dairy Development Board of India. We often noticed and commented on this advertisement because it was usually very creative and cleverly worded, and a new one was put up every few months. Over 20 years later, Amul butter still advertised from the same spot. But numerous other billboards had also sprung up in the area advertising both Indian and foreign consumer products, such as Pepsi, AT&T, Sony, McDonald's, Videocon, as well as cars, refrigerators, TVs, washing machines, and so forth. This is but one symbol of the continuation of the old and the incorporation of much that is new in India.

Looking back over thousands of years of Indian history, we see a civilization that has always been diverse and dynamic. Indigenous social and cultural practices have continuously interacted with external influences to shape its course. As Gita Mehta notes, ". . . at its best the culture of India is like a massive sponge, absorbing everything while purists shake their heads in despair . . . but India has always shown an appetite for foreign devils matched only by her capacity to make them go native" (1997:32). In this concluding chapter, I will reflect on some aspects of social change in modern India, and note some key challenges it faces as it enters the 21st century.

SOCIOLOGY AND SOCIAL CHANGE

Sociologists usually define **social change** as "any significant alteration, modification, or transformation" in the way a society is organized or operates (Ferrante 1998:470). All known human societies have experienced change, although the pace of change varies from one society to another, and from one part of society to another. Some changes may be planned or intended; others may be unplanned or unintended. Similarly, the nature and direction of change varies from place to place, and over time. Some people may view some changes as beneficial, and others as detrimental, to their lives. Human beings, however, are not just impacted by change, but are also the key agents of change in society. In the course of their everyday lives and work, and through social movements, they develop and spread new ideas, practices, tools, and technologies, compete for or come into conflict over valued resources, and engage in a variety of activities to reproduce existing patterns and to modify them.

Sociologists have developed two main theoretical frameworks to understand change in the contemporary world, **modernization theory,** and the **world system theory** (Bradshaw and Wallace 1996:39–57; Wallerstein 1974). Both theories have been used to understand social change in India, but both are found wanting. Social changes in India and elsewhere transcend both, but understanding the assumptions behind each theory helps assess social processes in India.

According to modernization theory, developed mainly in North America in the post-Second World War period, the key to development and progress in the mainly agricultural societies in Asia, Africa, and Latin America, was industrialization and technological development and related changes in political and social arrangements and human values. Western industrialized societies were presented as the model of the good society, and the less industrialized societies were viewed as backward. In

This photo gives a glimpse of the variety of modes of transportation and commercial ventures that can be seen on the streets of Indian cities.

addition to being ethnocentric, this model also assumed that industrialization necessarily leads to positive changes for everyone. Non-Western societies, in this view, would develop with the help of the more industrialized countries, or they would be able to do so on their own.

The world system theory, however, argues that all countries of the world are connected as part of the capitalist economic system in which the economic dominance of the industrialized countries is based upon exploitation of the less industrialized countries. As a result of colonization and the growth of multinational corporations based in the industrialized countries, the less industrialized countries became the source of raw materials and cheap labor, with productive assets and profits concentrated in the industrialized regions. The lack of development of a manufacturing base in the less developed regions, in this view, makes it almost impossible for them to catch up with the more developed regions even if they want to, or are expected to. The world system theory has been criticized for placing too much of the blame for the economic, political, and social problems in the less industrialized areas on the West, when in fact a variety of factors internal and external to the less developed regions interact to affect them.

Both theories, however, view social change as a result of the connection between the more and less economically developed regions of the world. In one case, through the spread of modernization from the Western countries to the non-Western regions, and in the other through domination and exploitation of the latter by the former. And in the last two decades, people all over the world have become increasingly connected economically, culturally, and politically as part of what is known as the process of **globalization.**

THE INDIAN CONTEXT

Many expected that with modernity, religion and caste in India would become less significant markers of identity and social action, and be replaced over time by the rational pursuit of individual self-interest and material well-being. Religious life in India, however, has never been static or homogeneous, and has always allowed appropriate space for economic pursuits. And religious faith in post-independence India has not been a barrier to industrial and technological changes. In fact, new commercial ventures are inaugurated with religious rituals! And modern communication technologies such as television, video and audio tapes, movies, books, and computers, have become an important means for the spread of religious ideas and practices, many of which reached only a limited audience until recently. Moreover, newer reinterpretations and constructions of religious traditions have become a significant part of social conflict and electoral politics in India, as illustrated in Chapters 3 and 8.

Caste hierarchies were also expected to disappear with modernization, and in fact during the nationalist movement and after independence, Indian leaders committed themselves to eliminating caste as the basis of inequality. However, as shown in Chapter 4, historically there has been a close connection between caste and economic inequalities. Also, it was possible to change caste and economic status. The British played a significant role in legitimizing caste hierarchies and Brahmanism. And while caste status is being increasingly delinked from economic status, like religion, caste has also become an important basis for political participation and social conflict in modern India. Moreover, caste as well as family status continue to be important in the conduct of daily life and in arranging marriages.

In the economic sphere, the Indian government emerged from British colonial domination with a firm commitment to modernization and industrialization, but without dependence on foreign aid or multinational corporations. India did succeed in developing a large internal industrial base and become self-sufficient in food production. But, as is clear from Chapter 5, the fruits of economic development have been spread unevenly, with significant areas of stagnation and large-scale poverty continuing. The Indian government has also loosened some regulations and controls over the economy, and there has been pressure to open up the Indian economy to foreign capital in recent years. Many fear, however, that economic liberalization and globalization will lead to greater dependence on foreign capital, and make India more vulnerable to global economic crises. A number of groups are organizing to resist liberalization, particularly the poor, small peasants, tribal groups, forest dwellers, women, and small entrepreneurs, whose lives and livelihoods are threatened by the power of foreign capital and big business. They are fighting for economic survival and social justice, and more local control of, and participation in, the development process.

Historically, there has been a considerable focus on appropriate gender roles in Indian as well as other societies. Chapter 6 presented the variety of images and roles of Indian women, as well as efforts to improve the status of women. Modern education and employment opportunities have improved the quality of life and status of many women. However, working-class and poor women have always been engaged in productive work to support their families, and paid employment often only adds to the work of caring for children and meeting household responsibilities. Moreover, commercialism and the desire for material goods associated with modernization have also increased the demands for dowry and violence against women. And new medical technologies are being used to determine the sex of the fetus and to abort many female fetuses. At the same time, though, India has one of the most active and diverse women's movements in the world working at different levels to promote gender equality.

Much attention has centered around marital arrangements and the joint family in India as traditionally conceived. Modern and Western influences were expected to increase the role of romantic love as the basis for marriage, and lead to the "breakdown" of the joint family. Although there is certainly more variation in the way marriages are arranged, families continue to play a major role in arranging marriages. And modern means of communication such as newspapers, magazines, and the Internet are used to place matrimonial advertisements. Household arrangements continue to be varied and diverse, but the joint family remains the ideal for most, and family obligations outweigh individualistic pursuits.

Modern formal education is viewed in India, as elsewhere, as the key to developing a trained workforce necessary for industrial, scientific, and technological development, as well as to improve the quality of life. And although India boasts of the third largest pool of scientists in the world, nearly half its population is illiterate, a disproportionate number of them being females, the poor, Dalits, and tribal populations. And not everyone is convinced that modern formal education imposed by the state from above is the best way to educate and empower people. Many argue for making education more responsive to the needs of the disadvantaged groups, and involving them in making decisions about the appropriate form of education necessary to improve their life chances.

India adopted a liberal-democratic political system based on the British parliamentary system to govern the country after independence. It is one of the few less industrialized non-Western countries to have regular elections, and is referred to as the world's largest democracy. However, electoral politics became an avenue not just for the expression and enhancement of individual aspirations and rights as in the West, but also the means to mobilize for the acquisition of power and resources on the basis of caste, class, religion, region, language, and gender. And in the last decade, no single party has been able to attain a majority in Parliament long enough to form a stable government, putting enormous pressure on the electoral system in the country. Moreover, the state has played a dominant role in regulating social and economic policy in India. Only in the last decade has state control been relaxed somewhat. A variety of community-based and other nongovernment organizations independent of the state and electoral politics have emerged as important parts of the political process in India. They often challenge dominant models of economic development and modernization, and have initiated debates on alternative models more suited to local needs and conditions.

It is clear from this overview that no single general model can explain social and cultural trends in India. Indian society has always been multidimensional and dynamic, and changes are also multidimensional. Multiple and often contradictory realities coexist, emerge, and change. New and old, foreign and indigenous forces interact to produce unique cultural blends that become part of the fabric of Indian society. I will give three examples from contemporary Indian popular culture to illustrate this notion.

CRICKET, FAST FOOD, AND CABLE TELEVISION

Reflecting on the popularity of the game of cricket in India, Ashis Nandy (1989:1) notes, "Cricket is an Indian game accidentally discovered by the British." In fact, the British introduced the game to India. The game is played using a bat, a ball, and wickets on two ends of a 22-yard-long pitch, with two teams of 11 members each. Cricket is believed to have influenced the development of baseball. Traditionally known as "the gentleman's game," cricket in Britain is a game of the elite introduced to the Western-oriented Indian elite and indeed associated with British imperialism. Gradually, however, particularly after independence, the sport became very popular in India, attaining a mass following, and is played by ordinary Indians. It has indeed become a national obsession and a medium for cultural expression, often arousing strong passions. Cricket, therefore, notes Nandy, is now more South Asian than British. People crowd into stadiums to watch, follow it live on TV, and listen to the radio commentary, children can be seen playing the game on the streets often using improvised bats, balls, and wickets, and businesses compete to sign on popular cricket players to sell products.

There was considerable excitement in urban India when McDonald's was introduced in 1996. Many see it as but one more example of the influence of American consumerism among the urban Indian elite and middle classes. However, as already noted at the beginning of this book, McDonald's accommodated to Indian tastes by excluding beef from its menu and by introducing many vegetarian items. Moreover, most Indians either cannot afford to eat at McDonald's or prefer the large variety of Indian fast foods that can be obtained anywhere from street vendors to upscale restaurants. McDonald's, therefore, has become part of a vast fast-food culture in India, rather than a replacement for Indian fast food!

The introduction of cable television in India in the late 1980s brought on CNN, MTV, and many other foreign TV channels showing American talk shows, sitcoms, and soap operas and raising fears of Western cultural invasion. Although many Indians are fascinated by foreign shows, over a period of time, programs produced by Indians on Indian themes have become more popular. MTV has accommodated to Indian tastes by extensively incorporating Indian popular music in its programming in order to compete with another music channel, V Channel, that also shows music videos combining Indian folk tunes with Western pop music, and music produced by Indian pop stars. Indian cable TV channels have become very popular, particularly those showing

Hindi movies and songs, as well as Indian sitcoms, current events, and social issues programs. Many of these programs are building on a long-standing and vibrant tradition of Indian popular music and film, and other forms of popular and folk expressions.

CONCLUSION

Although India displays a capacity to absorb great variety and difference, India's vastness, diversity, and complexity also contribute to numerous challenges. In spite of many technological and industrial achievements, poverty and illiteracy remain widespread. These forms of deprivation are closely connected to class, caste, and gender inequalities. Many social movements have emerged to bring about change. But mobilization along lines of caste, class, region, religion, tribe, and gender also make India a very tough country to govern and manage. And although population growth has slowed somewhat, the size of India's population is not expected to stabilize for another few decades, resulting in continuing stress on its resources. Population pressure plus industrialization, commercial agriculture, and forestry have resulted in enormous environmental pollution and degradation. Somehow, India still manages to survive as do most Indians. And even though India's problems often seem overwhelming, and it is impossible to predict the future with any degree of certainty, India offers too large a chunk of humanity to ignore.

GLOSSARY

Adi Granth   the holy book of the Sikhs.

Ahimsa   non-violence.

Ashrafs   Muslims in India who claim to be descendents of Muslims of foreign origin.

Bhagavad Gita   a text that forms part of the Hindu epic *Mahabharata* and contains the main beliefs and philosophies of Hinduism.

Bhakti   a form of worship based on devotion.

Bigamy   being married to more than one person at the same time.

Brahma   one of the three main Gods representing the Divine Principle in Hinduism, symbolized as the creator.

Brahmans   members of the highest caste in India, traditionally mainly priests and scholars.

Bride wealth or **bride price**   payment made by the groom's family to the bride's family in exchange for receiving the bride into his family.

Capitalism   an economic system in which resources and means of producing goods and services are privately owned.

Caste system   the classification of people into four hierarchically ranked, and hereditary, occupational groups as the basis of social status and access to power and resources.

Class system of stratification   social rank based on economic status related to ownership or nonownership of wealth and property or based on occupation and skill level.

Closed system of stratification   ranking based on a person's social status conferred by birth, very difficult to change, with limits on interaction with persons of another category.

Communalism   the term used for political action on the basis of religious or ethnic identity in India.

Core economies   countries whose economies are characterized by a high level of industrialization and mechanization, occupational diversification and stable governments.

Cult of true womanhood   an ideology stating that the ideal role of woman is as a full-time homemaker and mother, a pursuit through which she finds joy and fulfillment.

Dalit   the term means "oppressed people" and is now used by those who were considered untouchables in India to express pride in their culture and identity, as well as resistance to exploitation.

Dharma   sacred duty expressed through a complex system of beliefs, rituals, and rules of conduct considered necessary to maintain the order of things in Hinduism.

Dowry   the payment of gifts and cash by the bride's family to the groom and his family at the time of arranging a marriage.

Economic reforms   reforms to allow more freedom for private enterprise and commerce, and less government regulation of the economy.

Endogamy   marriage allowed only within the same social group, such as caste or religion.

Exogamy   marriage allowed outside a particular social category, such as clan, descent group, or village.

Extended family   members of a family who share close kinship ties, place expectations upon one another, are obligated to perform roles necessary for the maintenance of the family, but may or may not live in the same household.

Formal sector   part of the economy that includes large-scale manufacturing and commercial services characterized by secure employment, higher wages, and benefits for the employees.

Gender   socially learned ideas about the appropriate roles, behaviors, and appearance for females and males.

Globalization   the process by which people all over the world are increasingly connected economically, culturally, and politically.

Harijans   literally meaning "people of god," a term used by Mohandas Gandhi to refer to those conventionally considered outcaste or untouchable in India.

Hindutva   the idea of the essential nature of Hinduism that forms the basis of the notion that India is a Hindu nation.

Hypergamy   a marital arrangement according to which a woman is married to a man from a higher status family but usually within the same caste.

Informal sector   part of the economy that includes agriculture and related occupations, and small enterprises, and is mostly characterized by poor working conditions, insecure employment, few benefits, or protective legislation.

Jajmani system   an institution of patron-client relations in which castes performing specialized occupations exchanged goods and services within the village.

Jati   the numerous sub-castes within each of the four main castes in India.

Jats   the dominant agricultural group among the Sikhs, originally believed to be a tribal group.

Jihad   righteous struggle in defense of the faith now often termed holy war in Islam.

Joint family   ideally, a household arrangement in which one or two married couples live with their married sons, unmarried children, and/or grandchildren.

Kanyadaan   the practice of giving the daughter as a gift to the husband and his family by the father of the bride at marriage.

Karma   actions or deeds related to the theory that the nature of one's actions in this life determines the status of a person reborn into in the next life.

Khalsa   the community of "pure ones" created by the 10th Sikh Guru, Gobind Singh, as defenders of the Sikh faith.

Khatris   the dominant trading and entrepreneurial group among the Sikhs, originally from the Kshatriya caste.

Kshatriyas members of the second ranked caste in India, traditionally mainly political leaders and warriors.

Laws of Manu a set of classical Hindu texts that prescribe appropriate behavior for Hindus.

Liberal democracy a political system associated with institutions of representative government, multiparty elections, separation of powers, individual freedom, and protection of various rights.

Lok Sabha or people's assembly that forms the lower house of the Indian Parliament.

Mahabharata a great Hindu epic.

Mahila Panchayats women's councils.

Mansabdari a system of administration established by the Mughals.

Matrilineal a system of family organization in which descent is traced through the female line.

Mazhabi the term used to describe some low-status artisan castes and Dalits among the Sikhs.

Modernization theory a theory of development that states that the key to development and progress in the mainly agricultural societies in Asia, Africa, and Latin America is through industrialization and technological development, and related changes in political and social arrangements and human values.

Moksha a spiritual salvation that liberates a person from the endless cycle of birth and death.

Multinational corporations companies that own and operate enterprises in more than one country.

Nation a group of people who share, or believe that they share, a common culture, sense of belonging, and varying degrees of political consciousness on the basis of one or more of language, religion, ancestry, and other shared experiences often in relation to a territorial region over which they may or may not have political control.

Nation-state the territorial boundaries of a state corresponding with the nationality or culture of its members.

Nationalism a movement of members of a nationality or cultural group to create a nation-state, or attain some degree of political autonomy, or even to create a sense of national identity.

Nirvana a state of true emancipation achieved through a release from the endless cycle of rebirth and freedom from suffering.

Non-Ashrafs Muslims in India who are descendents of Muslims who converted to Islam as a consequence of Muslim rule in India.

Nonformal education alternative forms of community-based education and literacy programs for children and adults in poor and deprived groups who miss out on formal schooling.

Non-government organizations private voluntary or nonprofit organizations that work on a variety of issues of concern to people, such as education, poverty, development, human rights, health, and the environment.

Nuclear family   a group composed of a married couple and their dependent children.

Open system of stratification   ranking based on a person's social status and conferred on the basis of individual talent and ability, making it possible to move up or down in social rank.

Other Backward Classes   the term used to describe the non-untouchable lower-caste members, mostly Shudras, whose "backwardness" is based on social and economic disadvantages, and on the basis of which, it is argued, they should be accorded special privileges in order to overcome deprivation and discrimination.

Panchayati Raj   rule of the local village and town councils through transferring more powers to them.

Panchayats   village and town councils in India.

Participatory democracy   a political system that allows equal opportunities for all categories of people to participate in decisions affecting all arenas of human life including work, community, and interpersonal relations, in addition to formal political institutions.

Patriarchy   male domination in society.

Patrilineal   descent traced along the male line.

Patrilocal   system in which the bride moves to reside with the groom and his family upon marriage.

Peripheral economies   countries whose economies are characterized by a low level of industrial and technological development, with an economy highly dependent on a single commodity.

Polyandry   the practice of a woman being married to more than one man at the same time.

Polygamy   a system of marriage allowing a person to have more than one spouse.

Polygyny   the practice of a man marrying more than one wife.

Prakriti   a force of nature which is untamed and undifferentiated.

Primary sector   part of the economy concerned with extraction of resources directly from the earth, such as agriculture, forestry, mining, quarrying, and fishing.

Public sector enterprises   companies that are owned and operated by the state.

Puja   prayers that are part of Hindu worship.

Puranas   a set of Hindu literary texts.

Purdah   the veiling or seclusion of women.

Purusa   the cosmic person representing male force or energy.

Purusasukta hymn   the Vedic hymn that states the ritual basis for the ranking of the four main castes in India.

Qur'an   the sacred text of Islam that contains the revelations of Allah received by the Prophet Muhammad.

Rajya Sabha   the council of states that forms the upper house of the Indian Parliament.

Ramayana   a great Hindu epic.

Sakti   energy and power that is the source of creativity and life.

Sanskritization   a process through which a low caste, tribe, or other group takes on the customs, rituals, beliefs, ideology, and style of life of a high caste.

Sati   the practice of burning of a widow on the funeral pyre of her dead husband prevalent in the past in some parts of India among some social groups.

Scheduled Castes   the caste groups considered untouchable who were placed by the British Government of India, and later the Government of Independent India, on a list of groups that would be accorded special privileges in order to overcome deprivation and discrimination.

Scheduled Tribes   the tribal groups who were placed by the British Government of India, and later the Government of Independent India, on a list of groups that would be accorded special privileges in order to overcome deprivation and discrimination.

Secondary sector   part of the economy concerned with processing materials into different products, such as through manufacturing, construction, and power generation.

Secularism   defined in the Indian context as a process whereby the state protects religious freedoms but does not interfere in the conduct of religious affairs.

Semiperipheral economies   countries whose economies fall in between the core and peripheral economies. While they provide a significant amount of raw materials to the core, they are also stable and diversified enough to be a potential market, source of cheap labor, and investment by corporations based in the core countries.

Sharia   Islamic laws that guide the conduct of personal and public life by Muslims.

Shiva   one of the three main gods representing the Divine Principle in Hinduism, symbolized as the destroyer and reproducer.

Shudras   members of the fourth-ranked caste in India, traditionally mainly laborers, peasants, servants, and artisans.

Social change   any significant alteration, modification, or transformation in the way a society is organized or operates.

Social mobility   the movement of people higher or lower in social status, such as caste and class.

Social movements   organized efforts to bring about some form of social change or to resist change.

Social stratification   systematic ranking of categories of people on the basis of unequal access to valued resources, such as wealth, income, power, and prestige.

Socialism   an economic system in which resources and means of production are collectively owned and usually controlled by the state.

Socialization   the process through which individuals learn the appropriate values and norms of the social group.

State   a territorial unit, such as a country, which is usually recognized as politically independent, and has sovereignty in governing and administering its affairs.

Sufism   a mystical form of Islam

Sunnah   the texts that contain the words and deeds of the Prophet Muhammad.

Sustainable development   a model of development that keeps the needs of local people and the environment as the central focus of development.

Tertiary sector   part of the economy concerned with the provision of goods and services such as trade, transportation, finance, communications, administration, and defense.

Transmigration of souls   the passage of the immortal soul from one living being to another as part of the cycle of birth, death, and rebirth.

Uniform Civil Code   a legal code applicable to all individuals regardless of religious or ethnic affiliation.

Untouchables   those who are at the bottom of the social hierarchy performing tasks that are considered unclean and menial, and are defined as outcastes.

Vaishyas   members of the third-ranked caste in India, traditionally mainly merchants and agriculturalists.

Varna   the term used to refer to the four main castes in India composed of the Brahmans, Kshatriyas, Vaishyas, and Shudras.

Vedas   the texts that contain the main philosophical beliefs of Hinduism, with the **Rig Veda** as the most important.

Vishnu   one of the three main gods representing the Divine Principle in Hinduism, symbolized as the preserver.

Westernization   changes in lifestyle associated with Western influences, particularly European and North American.

World system theory   a theory of development that states that all countries of the world are connected as part of the capitalist economic system in which the economic dominance of the industrialized countries is based upon exploitation of the less industrialized countries.

Zamindar   a term used to describe a landholder.

INTERNET RESOURCES

There are numerous web sites that provide information about India. You can do a search using "India." Information on India can also be found under "South Asia" and "Asia." Listed below are some useful and interesting web sites and links.

1. These search engines provide links to web sites on a variety of topics relating to India.

   http://www.southasia.net/india/
   http://www.mahesh.com
   http://www.yahoo.com
   http://SunSITE.sut.ac.jp/asia/india

2. This is the web site for the Center for South Asia, University of Wisconsin, Madison. The Center supports teaching, research, and outreach relating to South Asia.

   http://www.wisc.edu/southasia

3. SARAI (South Asia Resources Access on the Internet): Columbia University. This web site provides information about resources, libraries, electronic journals, newspapers, etc., about South Asia by country and topic.

   http://www.columbia.edu/cu/libraries/indiv/area/sarai/

4. Asian Studies World Wide Web Virtual Library, Australian National University, includes information by individual country.

   http://coombs.anu.edu.au/WWWVL-AsianStudies.html

5. American Institute for Indian Studies is a consortium of universities and colleges in the United States linking scholars engaged in teaching and research about India. The web site also provides links to other resources.

   http://humanities.uchicago.edu/orgs/aiis/

6. South Asian Books from Missouri supplies South Asian publications.

   http://www.southasiabooks.com

7. The web site for the Government of India has information on a variety of topics, such as, culture, politics, economy, social issues, sports, media, science, and technology.

   http://india.indiagov.org/

8. Key statistics from the Census of India can be obtained from this web site.

   http://www.censusindia.net/

9. Sawnet (South Asian Women's NETwork) is a forum for those interested in South Asian women's issues. It contains links to information on a variety of topics, including women's organizations, books, journals, films, legal issues, domestic violence, electronic resources, etc.

   http://www.umiacs.umd.edu:80/users/sawweb/sawnet

10. The Indian Economic Overview web site has information on the Indian economy.

    http://www.ieo.org/

11. This web site has links to sites for Indian television and radio, music, newspapers, and magazines.

    http://SunSITE.sut.ac.jp/asia/india/media/

BIBLIOGRAPHY

Agarwal, Bina. *A Field of One's Own: Gender and Land Rights in South Asia.* Cambridge: Cambridge University Press, 1994.

Ahmed, Imtiaz. "Endogamy and Status Mobility among Siddique Sheikhs of Allahabad." In Dipankar Gupta (ed.), *Social Stratification.* Delhi: Oxford University Press, [1973] 1991, pp. 213–24.

Ahmed, Imtiaz. *Ritual and Religion among Muslims in India.* Columbia, Mo.: South Asia Books, 1982.

Ahmed, Imtiaz, ed. *Family, Kinship and Marriage among Muslims in India.* Columbia, Mo.: South Asia Books, 1976.

Amato, Paul R. "The Impact of Divorce on Men and Women in India and the United States." *Journal of Comparative Family Studies,* summer 1994.

Ansari, Javed. "Women's Reservation Bill: Casting Gender Aside." *India Today,* December 28, 1998.

Arcaro, Thomas E. "Social Change in Rural India: The Case of the Comprehensive Rural Health Project in Jamkhed, India." Unpublished manuscript, 1992.

Austin, Granville. "The Constitution, Society, and Law." In Philip Oldenburg (ed.), *India Briefing, 1993.* Boulder: Westview Press, 1993, pp. 103–29.

Bagchi, Amiya Kumar. "Dialectics of Indian Planning." In T. V. Sathyamurthy (ed.), *Industry and Agriculture in India since Independence.* Delhi: Oxford University Press, 1995, pp. 46–93.

Bagchi, Amiya Kumar. "Taxing the Poor to Pay the Rich." In Arun Kumar (ed.), *Structural Adjustment Policies: Loss of Sovereignty and Alternatives.* Lokayan Bulletin Special Issue. Delhi: Lokayan, 1991, pp. 32–36.

Banerjee, Nirmala, ed. *Indian Women in a Changing Industrial Scenario.* New Delhi: Sage Publications, 1991.

Bardhan, Pranab. "Dominant Proprietary Classes and India's Democracy." In Atul Kohli (ed.), *India's Democracy: An Analysis of Changing State-Society Relations.* Cambridge: Cambridge University Press, 1988, pp. 214–24.

Bardhan, Pranab. *The Political Economy of Development in India.* Oxford: Basil Blackwell, 1984.

Baru, Sanjaya. "Continuity and Change in Indian Industrial Policy." In T. V. Sathyamurthy (ed.), *Industry and Agriculture in India since Independence.* Delhi: Oxford University Press, 1995, pp. 115–34.

Basham, A. L. *The Origins and Development of Classical Hinduism.* Boston: Beacon Press, 1989.

Basu, Amrita, and Atul Kohli, eds. *Community Conflicts and the State in India.* Oxford: Oxford University Press, 1998.

Baxter, Craig, et al. *Government and Politics in South Asia.* 2d ed. Boulder: Westview Press, 1991.

Berreman, Gerald D. "Himalayan Polyandry and the Domestic Cycle." In Patricia Uberoi (ed.), *Family, Kinship and Marriage in India.* Delhi: Oxford University Press, [1975] 1993, pp. 257–72.

Berreman, Gerald D. "Chipko: A Movement to Save the Himalayan Environment and People." In Carla M. Borden (ed.), *Contemporary India: Essays on the Uses of Tradition*. Delhi: Oxford University Press, 1989, pp. 239–66.

Beteille, Andre. "Caste in Contemporary India." In C. J. Fuller (ed.), *Caste Today*. Delhi: Oxford University Press, 1996, pp. 150–226.

Beteille, Andre. *The Backward Classes in Contemporary India*. Delhi: Oxford University Press, 1992.

Bhargava, Ashok. "Agriculture." In James Heitzman and Robert L. Worden (eds.), *India: A Country Study*. Washington, D.C.: Federal Research Division, Library of Congress, 1996, pp. 379–428.

Bhatty, Kiran. "Educational Deprivation in India: A Survey of Field Investigations." *Economic and Political Weekly*, July 4, 1998, pp. 1731–40, and July 11, 1998, pp. 1858–69.

Bhatty, Zarina. "Social Stratification among Muslims in India." In M. N. Srinivas (ed.), *Caste: Its Twentieth Century Avatar*. Delhi: Viking, 1996, pp. 244–62.

Bose, Sugata, and Ayesha Jalal. *Modern South Asia: History, Culture, Political Economy*. London and New York: Routledge, 1998.

Bose, Sugata, and Ayesha Jalal, eds. *Nationalism, Democracy and Development: State and Politics in India*. Delhi: Oxford University Press, 1997.

Bougle, C. "The Essence and Reality of the Caste System." In Dipankar Gupta, (ed.), *Social Stratification*. Delhi: Oxford University Press, [1958] 1991, pp. 64–73.

Bouton, Marshall M. "Foreign Relations: Elusive Regional Security." In Marshall M. Bouton (ed.), *India Briefing, 1987*. Boulder: Westview Press, 1987, pp. 159–83.

Bradshaw, York W., and Michael Wallace. *Global Inequalities*. Thousand Oaks, Calif.: Pine Forge Press, 1996.

Brass, Paul R. *The Politics of India Since Independence*. 2d ed. Cambridge: Cambridge University Press, 1994.

Brass, Paul R. "The Punjab Crisis and the Unity of India." In Atul Kohli (ed.), *India's Democracy: An Analysis of Changing State–Society Relations*. Cambridge: Cambridge University Press, 1988, pp. 169–213.

Butalia, Urvashi, *The Other Side of Silence: Voices from the Partition of India*. New Delhi: Penguin Books, 1998.

Caplan, Lionel. "Bridegroom Price in Urban India: Caste, Class and 'Dowry Evil' among Christians in India." In Patricia Uberoi (ed.), *Family, Kinship and Marriage in India*. Delhi: Oxford University Press, [1984] 1993, pp. 357–79.

Chanana, Karuna. "Social Change or Social Reform: The Education of Women in Pre-Independence India." In A. M. Shah et al. (eds.), *Women in Indian Society*. New Delhi: Sage Publications, 1996, pp. 113–48.

Chanana, Karuna, ed. *Socialization, Education and Women: Explorations in Gender Identity*. Delhi: Orient Longman, 1988.

Chatterji, P. C. "Reservation: Theory and Practice." In T. V. Sathyamurthy (ed.), *Region, Religion, Caste, Gender and Culture in Contemporary India*. Delhi: Oxford University Press, 1996, pp. 293–313.

Chaudhuri, Pramit. "Economic Planning in India." In T. V. Sathyamurthy (ed.), *Industry and Agriculture in India since Independence*. Delhi: Oxford University Press, 1995, pp. 94–114.

Cohen, Stephen Philip. "India as a Great Power: Perceptions and Prospects." In Philip Oldenburg (ed.), *India Briefing, 1991.* Boulder: Westview Press, 1991, pp. 75–95.

Damodaran, Ashok K., and Javed M. Ansari. "Bihar: Rubbed Out." *India Today,* 22, February 1999, pp. 19–22.

Dandekar, V. M. *The Indian Economy: 1947–92.* Vol. I. New Delhi: Sage Publications, 1994.

Dasgupta, Jyotirindra. "Community, Authenticity and Autonomy: Insurgence and Institutional Development in India's North-East." In Amrita Basu and Atul Kohli (eds.), *Community Conflicts and the State in India.* Delhi: Oxford University Press, 1998, pp. 183–214.

Das Gupta, Jyotirindra. "Ethnicity, Democracy and Development in India: Assam in a General Perspective." In Atul Kohli (ed.), *India's Democracy: An Analysis of Changing State–Society Relations.* Cambridge: Cambridge University Press, 1988, pp. 144–68.

Datta, Bishakha, ed. *"And Who Will Make the Chapatis?": A Study of All-Women Panchayats in Maharashtra.* Calcutta: Stree, 1998.

Davis, Richard H. "Introduction." In Donald S. Lopez, Jr. (ed.), *Religions of India in Practice.* Princeton: Princeton University Press, 1995, pp. 3–52.

Desai, Meghnad. "Economic Reform: Stalled by Politics?" In Philip Oldenburg (ed.), *India Briefing: Staying the Course.* Armonk, N.Y.: M. E. Sharpe, 1995, pp. 75–95.

Desai, Neera. "Women's Employment and Their Familial Role in India." In A. M. Shah et al. (eds.), *Women in Indian Society.* New Delhi: Sage Publications, 1996, pp. 98–112.

Dhanagare, D. N. "The Model of Agrarian Classes in India." In Dipankar Gupta, (ed.), *Social Stratification.* Delhi: Oxford University Press, [1983] 1991, pp. 271–75.

Dhillon, Amrit, and Harinder Baweja. "Women's Reservation Bill: An Agenda for Empowerment." *India Today,* October 15, 1996, pp. 46–49.

Dreze, Jean, and Amartya Sen. *India: Economic Development and Social Opportunity.* Delhi: Oxford University Press, 1995.

Dube, Leela. "Caste and Women." In M. N. Srinivas (ed.), *Caste: Its Twentieth Century Avatar.* Delhi: Viking, 1996, pp. 1–27.

Dube, Leela. "Socialization of Hindu Girls in Patrilineal India." In Karuna Chanana (ed.), *Socialization, Education and Women: Explorations in Gender Identity.* Delhi: Orient Longman, 1988, pp. 166–92.

Dube, Saurabh. *Untouchable Pasts: Religion, Identity, and Power among a Central Indian Community, 1780–1950.* Albany: State University of New York Press, 1998.

Dutt, Ashok K., and M. Margaret Geib. *Atlas of South Asia.* Boulder: Westview Press, 1987.

Embree, Ainslie T. *Utopias in Conflict: Essays on Indian History.* Berkeley: University of California Press, 1990.

Epstein, T. Scarlett. "Culture, Women and India's Development." In A. M. Shah et al. (eds.), *Women in Indian Society.* New Delhi: Sage Publications, 1996, pp. 33–55.

Ferrante, Joan. *Sociology: A Global Perspective.* 3d ed. Belmont, Calif.: Wadsworth Publishing Company, 1998.

Forbes, Geraldine. *Women in Modern India.* Cambridge: Cambridge University Press, 1996.

Frankel, Francine R. "Introduction." In Francine R. Frankel and M. S. A. Rao (eds.), *Dominance and State Power in Modern India.* Vol. I. Delhi: Oxford University Press, 1989, pp. 1–20.

Frankel, Francine R. *India's Political Economy: 1947–1977.* Delhi: Oxford University Press, 1978.

Frankel, Francine R., and M. S. A. Rao, eds. *Dominance and State Power in India.* Vol. II. Delhi: Oxford University Press, 1990.

Frankel, Francine R., and M. S. A. Rao, eds. *Dominance and State Power in Modern India.* Vol. I. Delhi: Oxford University Press, 1989.

French, Patrick. "The New Gandhi." *The New Yorker,* March 16, 1998, pp. 36–44.

Fuller, C. J. *The Camphor Flame: Popular Hinduism and Society in India.* Princeton: Princeton University Press, 1992.

Fuller, C. J., ed. *Caste Today.* Delhi: Oxford University Press, 1996.

Fuller, C. J. "Kerala Christians and the Caste System." In Dipankar Gupta (ed.), *Social Stratification.* Delhi: Oxford University Press, 1991, pp. 195–212.

Galanter, Marc. *Competing Inequalities: Law and the Backward Classes in India.* Berkeley: University of California Press, 1983.

Gandhi, Nandita, and Nandita Shah. *The Issues at Stake: Theory and Practice in the Contemporary Women's Movement in India.* New Delhi: Kali for Women, 1991.

Ghurye, G. S. "Features of the Caste System." In Dipankar Gupta (ed.), *Social Stratification.* Delhi: Oxford University Press, [1969] 1991, pp. 35–48.

Gough, E. Kathleen. "Brahman Kinship in a Tamil Village." In Patricia Uberoi (ed.), *Family, Kinship and Marriage in India.* Delhi: Oxford University Press, [1956] 1993, pp. 146–75.

Gough, E. Kathleen. "The Nayars and the Definition of Marriage." In Patricia Uberoi (ed.), *Family, Kinship and Marriage in India.* Delhi: Oxford University Press, [1959] 1993, pp. 237–56.

Goyal, Santosh. "Social Background of Indian Corporate Executives." In Francine R. Frankel and M. S. A. Rao (eds.), *Dominance and State Power in India.* Vol. II. Delhi: Oxford University Press, 1990, pp. 535–44.

Goyal, Santosh. "Social Background of Officers in the Indian Administrative Service." In Francine R. Frankel and M. S. A. Rao (eds.), *Dominance and State Power in Modern India.* Vol. I. Delhi: Oxford University Press, 1989, pp. 425–33.

Gupta, Dipankar, ed. *Social Stratification.* Delhi: Oxford University Press, 1991*a*.

Gupta, Dipankar. "Continuous Hierarchies and Discrete Castes." In Dipankar Gupta (ed.), *Social Stratification.* Delhi: Oxford University Press, 1991*b*, pp. 110–41.

Gupta, S. P. "Recent Economic Reforms in India and Their Impact on the Poor and Vulnerable Sections of Society." In C. H. Hanumantha Rao and Hans Linnemann (eds.), *Economic Reforms and Poverty Alleviation in India.* New Delhi: Sage Publications, 1996, pp. 126–70.

Haider, Saraswati. "An Ethnographic Profile of Family and Kinship among Eastern Uttar Pradesh Chamar Migrants in a Delhi Squatter Settlement." *Guru Nanak Journal of Sociology* 18, no. 2 (October 1997a): 1–32.

Haider, Sarawati. "National Policy for Women in India 1996—A Critique." *Social Scientist,* Vol. 25, Nos. 3–4, March–April 1997b: 38–64.

Haider, Saraswati. "National Policy for Women." *Lokayan Bulletin* 13, no. 2 (1996): 17–26.

Hasan, Mushirul. "The Changing Position of Muslims and the Political Future of Secularism in India." In T. V. Sathyamurthy (ed.), *Region, Religion, Caste, Gender and Culture in Contemporary India.* Delhi: Oxford University Press, 1996, pp. 200–28.

Hasan, Zoya. "Gender Politics, Legal Reform, and the Muslim Community in India." In Patricia Jeffery and Amrita Basu (eds.), *Appropriating Gender: Women's Activism and Politicized Religion in South Asia.* New York: Routledge, 1998, pp. 71–88.

Heitzman, James, and Robert L. Worden, eds. *India: A Country Study.* Washington, D.C.: Federal Research Division, Library of Congress, 1996.

Heston, Alan. "Poverty in India: Some Recent Policies." In Marshall M. Bouton and Philip Oldenburg (eds.), *India Briefing, 1990.* Boulder: Westview Press, 1990, pp. 101–28.

Horowitz, Irving Louis. *C. Wright Mills: An American Utopian.* New York: The Free Press, 1983.

Ilaiah, Kancha. "Productive Labour, Consciousness and History: The Dalitbahujan Alternative." In Shahid Amin and Dipesh Chakrabarty (eds.), *Subaltern Studies IX: Writings on South Asian History and Society.* Delhi: Oxford University Press, 1997, pp. 165–200.

Ilaiah, Kancha. *Why I Am Not a Hindu.* Calcutta: Samya, 1996.

India Today. " India: State of the Nation." August 18, 1997:24–35.

India Today. "The Maturing of a Democracy." August 31, 1996:28–43.

Jayaram, N. "Caste and Hinduism: Changing Protean Relationship." In M. N. Srinivas (ed.), *Caste. Its Twentieth Century Avatar.* Delhi: Viking, 1996, pp. 69–86.

Jeffery, Patricia, and Amrita Basu, eds. *Appropriating Gender: Women's Activism and Politicized Religion in South Asia.* New York: Routledge, 1998.

Joshi, Charu Lata. "Women in Panchayats: Crossing the Threshold." *India Today,* May 15, 1995, pp. 92–95.

Kappen, S. "Towards an Alternative Cultural Paradigm of Development." *Lokayan Bulletin* 10, no. 4, (January–February 1994):5–14.

Karanth, G. K. "Caste in Contemporary Rural India." In M. N. Srinivas (ed.), *Caste: Its Twentieth Century Avatar.* Delhi: Viking, 1996, pp. 87–109.

Karlekar, Malavika. "Domestic Violence." *Economic and Political Weekly,* July 4, 1998, pp. 1741–51.

Karve, Irawati. "The Kinship Map of India." In Patricia Uberoi (ed.), *Family, Kinship and Marriage in India.* Delhi: Oxford University Press, [1953] 1993, pp. 50–73.

Khanna, Sunil. "Prenatal Sex Determination: A New Family-Building Strategy." *Manushi,* no. 86 (January–February 1995): 23–29.

Kishwar, Madhu. "A Half Step Forward: The Thwarting of Economic Reforms in India." *Manushi,* nos. 92–93 (January–April 1996): 51–80.

Kishwar, Madhu. "Out of the Zanana Dabba: Strategies for Enhancing Women's Political Representation." *Manushi,* no. 96 (September–October 1996): 21–30.

Kishwar, Madhu. "When Daughters Are Unwanted: Sex Determination Tests in India." *Manushi,* no. 86 (January–February 1995): 15–22.

Kishwar, Madhu. "Stimulating Reform, Not Forcing it: Uniform Versus Optional Civil Code." *Manushi*, no. 89 (July–August 1995): 5–14.

Kishwar, Madhu. "Breaking the Stalemate: Uniform Civil Code vs. Personal Laws." *Manushi*, no. 77 (July–August 1993):2–5.

Kishwar, Madhu. *Gandhi and Women*. Delhi: Manushi Prakashan, 1986.

Kishwar, Madhu, and Ruth Vanita. "Indian Women: A Decade of New Ferment." In Marshall M. Bouton and Philip Oldenburg (eds.), *India Briefing, 1989*. Boulder: Westview Press, 1989, pp. 131–51.

Kohli, Atul. *Democracy and Discontent: India's Growing Crisis of Governability*. Cambridge: Cambridge University Press, 1990.

Kohli, Atul, ed. *India's Democracy: An Analysis of Changing State–Society Relations*. Cambridge: Cambridge University Press, 1988.

Kothari, Rajni. *Politics and the People: In Search of a Humane India*. Delhi: Ajanta Publications, 1990.

Kothari, Rajni. *State Against Democracy: In Search of Humane Governance*. Delhi: Ajanta Publications, 1989.

Kothari, Smitu. "Social Movements and the Redefinition of Democracy." In Philip Oldenburg (ed.), *India Briefing, 1993*. Boulder: Westview Press, 1993, pp. 131–62.

Kothari, Smitu, ed. *Dams on the River Narmada: A Call to Conscience*. Delhi: *Lokayan Bulletin*, 1991.

Kumar, Arun, ed. *Structural Adjustment Policies: Loss of Sovereignty and Alternatives. Lokayan Bulletin*, Special Issue. Delhi: Lokayan, 1991.

Kumar, Radha. "From Chipko to Sati: The Contemporary Indian Women's Movement." In Amrita Basu (ed.), *The Challenge of Local Feminisms: Women's Movements in Global Perspective*. Boulder: Westview, 1995a, pp. 58–86.

Kumar, Radha. "Political Women and Women's Politics in India." In Alida Brill (ed.), *A Rising Public Voice: Women in Politics Worldwide*. New York: The Feminist Press, 1995b, pp. 59–72.

Kundu, Amitabh. "New Economic Policy and Urban Poverty in India." In C. H. Hanumantha Rao and Hans Linnemann (eds.), *Economic Reforms and Poverty Alleviation in India*. New Delhi: Sage Publications, 1996, pp. 199–227.

Liddle, Joanna, and Rama Joshi. *Daughters of Independence: Gender, Caste and Class in India*. New Brunswick, N.J.: Rutgers University Press, 1989.

Lipset, Seymour Martin. *American Exceptionalism: A Double-Edged Sword*. New York: W. W. Norton, 1996.

Macpherson, C. B. *The Real World of Democracy*. Toronto: Canadian Broadcasting Corporation, 1966.

Madan, T. N. "The Hindu Family and Development." In Patricia Uberoi (ed.), *Family, Kinship and Marriage in India*. Delhi: Oxford University Press, [1976] 1993, pp. 416–34.

Madan, T. N. "The Structural Implications of Marriage in North India: Wife-givers and Wife-takers among the Pandits of Kashmir." In Patricia Uberoi (ed.), *Family, Kinship and Marriage in India*. Delhi: Oxford University Press, [1975] 1993, pp. 287–306.

Madan, T. N. "Secularism in Its Place." In T. N. Madan (ed.), *Religion in India*. New York: Oxford University Press, 1992, pp. 394–409.

Mahanta, Aparna. "The Indian State and Patriarchy." In T. V. Sathyamurthy (ed.), *State and Nation in the Context of Social Change.* Delhi: Oxford University Press, 1994, pp. 87–131.

Manor, James. "Parties and the Party System." In Atul Kohli (ed.), *India's Democracy: An Analysis of Changing State–Society Relations.* Cambridge: Cambridge University Press, 1988, pp. 62–98.

Mathur, K. S. "Hindu Values of Life: Karma and Dharma." In T. N. Madan (ed.), *Religion in India.* New York: Oxford University Press, 1992, pp. 62–77.

Mayer, Adrian. "Caste in an Indian Village: Change and Continuity, 1954–1992." In C. J. Fuller (ed.), *Caste Today.* Delhi: Oxford University Press, 1996, pp. 32–64.

McLeod, W. H. *The Sikhs: History, Religion, and Society.* New York: Columbia University Press, 1989.

Mehta, Gita. *Snakes and Ladders: Glimpses of Modern India.* New York: Doubleday, 1997.

Mencher, Joan P. "South Indian Female Cultivators:Who They Are and What They Do?" In A. M. Shah et al. (eds.), *Women in Indian Society.* New Delhi: Sage Publications, 1996, pp. 56–78.

Mies, Maria. *The Lace Makers of Narsapur: Indian Housewives Produce for the World Market.* London: Zed Press, 1982.

Mukhopadhyay, Carol Chapnick, and Susan Seymour, eds. *Women, Education, and Family Structure in India.* Boulder: Westview Press, 1994.

Nandy, Ashis. *The Tao of Cricket: On Games of Destiny and the Destiny of Games.* New Delhi: Penguin Books, 1989.

Narang, Amarjit Singh. *Democracy, Development and Distortion: Punjab Politics in National Perspective.* New Delhi: Gitanjali Publishing House, 1988.

Nath, Meenakshi. "Cutting Across Party Lines: Women Members of Parliament Explain Their Stand on Reservation Quotas." *Manushi,* no. 96 (September–October 1996): 7–16.

Navlakha, Gautam. "Invoking Union: Kashmir and Official Nationalism of 'Bharat.' " In T. V. Sathyamurthy (ed.), *Region, Religion, Caste, Gender and Culture in Contemporary India.* Delhi: Oxford University Press, 1996, pp. 64–106.

Nayyar, Rohini. "New Initiatives for Poverty Alleviation in Rural India." In C. H. Hanumantha Rao and Hans Linnemann (eds.), *Economic Reforms and Poverty Alleviation in India.* New Delhi: Sage Publications, 1996, pp. 171–98.

Nongbri, Tiplut. "Gender and the Khasi Family Structure." In Patricia Uberoi (ed.), *Family, Kinship and Marriage in India.* Delhi: Oxford University Press, [1988] 1993, pp. 176–86.

Omvedt, Gail. "The Anti-Caste Movement and the Discourse of Power." In T. V. Sathyamurthy (ed.), *Region, Religion, Caste, Gender and Culture in Contemporary India.* Delhi: Oxford University Press, 1996, pp. 334–54.

Omvedt, Gail. *Reinventing Revolution: New Social Movements and the Socialist Tradition in India.* Armonk, N.Y.: M. E. Sharpe, 1993.

Omvedt, Gail. *Violence Against Women: New Movements and New Theories in India.* New Delhi: Kali for Women, 1990.

Palriwala, Rajni, and Indu Agnihotri. "Tradition, the Family, and the State: Politics of the Contemporary Women's Movement." In T. V. Sathyamurthy (ed.), *Region, Religion, Caste, Gender and Culture in Contemporary India.* Delhi: Oxford University Press, 1996, pp. 503–32.

Pandey, Shashi Ranjan. *Community Action for Social Justice: Grassroots Organizations in India.* New Delhi: Sage, 1991.

Parry, Geraint, and Michael Moran, eds. *Democracy and Democratization.* London: Routledge, 1994.

Pateman, Carole. *Participation and Democratic Theory.* Cambridge: Cambridge University Press, 1970.

Patnaik, Arun, and K. S. R. V. S. Chalam. "The Ideology and Politics of Hindutva." In T. V. Sathyamurthy (ed.), *Region, Religion, Caste, Gender and Culture in Contemporary India.* Delhi: Oxford University Press, 1996, pp. 252–80.

Ragin, Charles, and David Zaret. "Theory and Method in Comparative Strategies." *Social Forces* 61(1983): 731–54.

Rao, M. S. A. "Some Conceptual Issues in the Study of Caste, Class, Ethnicity and Dominance." In Francine R. Frankel and M. S. A. Rao (eds.), *Dominance and State Power in Modern India.* Vol. I. Delhi: Oxford University Press, 1989, pp. 21–45.

Ramaswamy, E. A. "Organized Labor and Economic Reform." In Philip Oldenburg (ed.), *India Briefing: Staying the Course.* Armonk, N.Y.: M. E. Sharpe, 1995, pp. 97–128.

Rogers, John D. "Character and Structure of the Economy." In James Heitzman and Robert L. Worden (eds.), *India: A Country Study.* Washington, D.C.: Federal Research Division, Library of Congress, 1996, pp. 295–358.

Rose, Kalima. *Where Women Are Leaders: The SEWA Movement in India.* London: Zed Books, 1992.

Rubenstein, James M. *The Cultural Landscape: An Introduction to Human Geography.* 6th ed. Upper Saddle River, N.J.: Prentice Hall, 1999.

Rubin, Barnett R. "Journey to the East: Industrialization in India and the Chinese Experience." In Dilip K. Basu and Richard Sisson (eds.), *Social and Economic Development in India: A Reassessment.* New Delhi: Sage Publications, 1986, pp. 67–88.

Sathyamurthy, T. V., ed. *Industry and Agriculture in India Since Independence.* Delhi: Oxford University Press, 1995.

Schmidt, Karl J. *An Atlas and Survey of South Asian History.* Armonk, N.Y.: M. E. Sharpe, 1995.

Schwartzberg, Joseph E. *South Asian Studies in American Higher Education.* Ann Arbor, Mich.: The Association for Asian Studies, 1989.

Sekhon, Joti. "Grassroots Social Action and Empowerment in India: The Case of Action India Women's Program." In Jill M. Bystydzienski and Joti Sekhon (eds.), *Democratization and Women's Grassroots Movements.* Bloomington: Indiana University Press, 1999, pp. 25–48.

Sen, Ilina. "Women's Politics in India." In T. V. Sathyamurthy (ed.), *Region, Religion, Caste, Gender and Culture in Contemporary India.* Delhi: Oxford University Press, 1996, pp. 444–62.

Sen, Ilina, ed. *A Space within the Struggle: Women's Participation in People's Movements.* New Delhi: Kali for Women, 1990.

Seymour, Susan C. *Women, Family, and Child Care in India: A World in Transition.* Cambridge: Cambridge University Press, 1999.

Seymour, Susan. "College Women's Aspirations: A Challenge to the Patrilocal Family System?" In Carol Chapnick Mukhopadhyay and Susan Seymour (eds.), *Women, Education, and Family Structure in India.* Boulder: Westview Press, 1994, pp. 213–33.

Shah, Ghanshyam. "Grass-Roots Mobilization in Indian Politics." In Atul Kohli (ed.), *India's Democracy: An Analysis of Changing State–Society Relations.* Cambridge: Cambridge University Press, 1988, pp. 262–304.

Sharma, Kumud. *Women in Struggle: Role and Participation of Women in the Chipko Movement.* New Delhi: Centre for Women's Development Studies, 1987.

Sharma, Ursula. "Dowry in North India: Its Consequences for Women." In Patricia Uberoi (ed.), *Family, Kinship and Marriage in India.* Delhi: Oxford University Press, [1984] 1993, pp. 341–56.

Sheth, D. L. "Changing Terms of Elite Discourse: The Case of Reservation for 'Other Backward Classes.' " In T. V. Sathyamurthy (ed.), *Region, Religion, Caste, Gender and Culture in Contemporary India.* Delhi: Oxford University Press, 1996, pp. 314–33.

Shiva, Vandana. *Staying Alive: Women, Ecology and Development.* London: Zed Books, 1989.

Shotton, John R. *Learning and Freedom: Policy, Pedagogy and Paradigms in Indian Education and Schooling.* New Delhi: Sage Publications, 1998.

Singh, Khushwant. *A History of the Sikhs.* Vol 2. Delhi: Oxford University Press, 1977.

Singh, Khushwant. *A History of the Sikhs.* Vol. 1. Delhi: Oxford University Press, 1963.

Singh, Simrita Gopal, et al. "Participation of Women in Electoral Politics in Maharashtra." In *Women in Politics: Forms and Processes.* New Delhi: Friedrich Ebert Stiftung, 1992, pp. 63–107.

Smelser, Neil J. *Comparative Methods in the Social Sciences.* Englewood Cliffs, N.J.: Prentice Hall, 1976.

Spear, Percival. *A History of India.* Vol. 2. London: Penguin Books, 1978.

Srinivas, M. N., ed. *Caste: Its Twentieth Century Avatar.* Delhi: Viking, 1996.

Srinivas, M. N. "Mobility in the Caste System." In Dipankar Gupta (ed.), *Social Stratification.* Delhi: Oxford University Press, [1989] 1991, pp. 313–25.

Srinivas, M. N. *Some Reflections on Dowry.* Delhi: Oxford University Press, 1984.

Srivastava, Ravi. "India's Uneven Development and Its Implications for Political Processes: An Analysis of Some Recent Trends." In T. V. Sathyamurthy (ed.), *Industry and Agriculture in India since Independence.* Delhi: Oxford University Press, 1995, pp. 219–47.

Suresh, V. "The Dalit Movement in India." In T. V. Sathyamurthy (ed.), *Region, Religion, Caste, Gender and Culture in Contemporary India.* Delhi: Oxford University Press, 1996, pp. 355–87.

Swaminathan, Mina, ed. *The First Five Years: A Critical Perspective on Early Childhood Care and Education in India.* New Delhi: Sage Publications, 1998.

Talbot, Phillips. "Kashmir's Agony." In Philip Oldenburg (ed.), *India Briefing, 1991.* Boulder: Westview Press, 1991, pp. 123–42.

Tandon, Rajesh. "Civil Society, the State and Roles of NGOs." Unpublished paper. New Delhi: Society for Participatory Research in Asia, 1991.

Thapar, Romila. "Traditions Versus Misconceptions." *Manushi,* nos. 42–43 (September–December 1987): pp. 2–14.

Thapar, Romila. *A History of India.* Vol. 1. London: Penguin Books, 1966.

Tharamangalam, J. "Caste among Christians in India." In M. N. Srinivas (ed.), *Caste: Its Twentieth Century Avatar.* Delhi: Viking, 1996, pp. 263–91.

Tharu, Susie, and K. Lalita, eds. *Women Writing in India: 600 B.C. to the Present.* Vol. I. New York: The Feminist Press, 1991.

Thomas, Bryn. *India.* Hawthorn, Australia: Lonely Planet, 1997.

Thorat, S. K. "Dalits and India's Independence." *Dalit International Newsletter* 3, no. 3 (October 1998).

Thorner, Daniel. *The Agrarian Prospect in India.* Delhi: Allied Publications, 1973.

The Times of India. "Panchayati raj raises political consciousness among women," November 26, 1997.

The Times of India. "GDP to grow by 5.8% in 1998–99." February 10, 1999.

The Times of India. "Rate of inflation rises marginally." February 1, 1999.

Uberoi, Patricia. "The Family in Official Discourse." In Geeti Sen and Susan Visvanathan (eds.), *Second Nature: Women and the Family.* India International Centre Quarterly, winter 1996, pp. 134–55.

Uberoi, Patricia, ed. *Family, Kinship and Marriage in India.* Delhi: Oxford University Press, 1993.

Ullrich, Helen E. "Asset and Liability: The Role of Female Education in Changing Marriage Patterns among Havik Brahmins." In Carol Chapnick Mukhopadhyay and Susan Seymour (eds.), *Women, Education, and Family Structure in India.* Boulder: Westview Press, 1994, pp. 187–212.

United Nations. *Population Change, Development and Women's Role and Status in India.* New York: United Nations, 1995.

United Nations. *The World's Women: Trends and Statistics 1970–1990.* New York: United Nations, 1991.

Vaidyanathan, A. "The Political Economy of the Evolution of Anti-Poverty Programmes." In T. V. Sathyamurthy (ed.), *Industry and Agriculture in India since Independence.* Delhi: Oxford University Press, 1995, pp. 329–47.

Varshney, Ashutosh. "Battling the Past, Forging a Future? Ayodhya and Beyond." In Philip Oldenburg (ed.), *India Briefing, 1993.* Boulder: Westview Press, 1993, pp. 9–42.

Vatuk, Sylvia. "Identity and Difference or Equality and Inequality in South Asian Muslim Society." In C. J. Fuller (ed.), *Caste Today.* Delhi: Oxford University Press, 1996, pp. 227–62.

Vatuk, Sylvia. "Making New Homes in the City: Urbanization and the Contemporary Indian Family." In Carla M. Borden (ed.), *Contemporary India: Essays on the Uses of Tradition.* Delhi: Oxford University Press, 1989, pp. 187–202.

Vishwanath, L. S. "Female Infanticide and the Position of Women in India." In A. M. Shah et. al. (eds.), *Women in Indian Society.* New Delhi: Sage Publications, 1996, pp. 179–205.

Wadley, Susan S., and Bruce W. Derr. "Karimpur Families over 60 years." In Patricia Uberoi (ed.), *Family, Kinship and Marriage in India.* Delhi: Oxford University Press, [1988] 1993, pp. 393–415.

Wadley, Susan. "Women and the Hindu Tradition." In Rehana Ghadially (ed.), *Women in Indian Society: A Reader.* New Delhi: Sage Publications, 1988, pp. 23–43.

Wallerstein, Immanual. *The Modern World–System.* New York: Academic Press, 1974.

Weiner, Myron. *The Child and the State in India: Child Labor and Education Policy in Comparative Perspective*. Princeton: Princeton University Press, 1991.

Weiner, Myron. *Sons of the Soil: Migration and Ethnic Conflict in India*. Princeton: Princeton University Press, 1978.

Widmalm, Sten. "The Rise and Fall of Democracy in Kashmir 1975–1989." In Amrita Basu and Atul Kohli (eds.), *Community Conflicts and the State in India*. Oxford: Oxford University Press, 1998, pp. 149–82.

Wolpert, Stanley. *A New History of India*. 4th ed. New York and Oxford: Oxford University Press, 1993.

World Bank. *World Development Report 1997*. Washington, D.C.: Oxford University Press, 1997.

INDEX

A

Adi Granth, 33
Agarwal, Bina, 80, 149
Agnihotri, Indu, 82, 155
agriculture, 2, 11, 14, 15, 17, 19, 20,
  52–53, 58, 59, 60, 61, 62–64, 66–67, 76,
  78–80, 123, 129
  during British period, 19, 20
  and caste, 52–53
  in early India, 14, 15
  and economy, 58, 59, 60, 61, 62–64
  farmer's movements, 129
  and gender, 76, 78–80
  in Mughal empire, 17
  and poverty, 66–67
  in Punjab, 123
ahimsa, 13, 32; *see also* non-violence
Ahmed, Imtiaz, 31, 46, 97, 149
Akali Dal, 118, 122, 123
Akbar, 16–17
All-India Muslim League, 21; *see also*
  Muslim League
Amato, Paul R., 102, 149
Ambedkar, B.R., 45, 48, 119
Ansari, Javed, 149, 151
anti-caste movement, 37, 48–49
Arcaro, Thomas E., 149
arranged marriage, 74, 93, 94, 138
art and architecture, 4
Ashrafs, 46
Austin, Granville, 114, 149

B

Bagchi, Amiya Kumar, 62, 70, 149
Bahujan Samaj Party, 49, 119
Banerjee, Nirmala, 81, 149
Bano, Shah, 37, 86–87
Bardhan, Pranab, 53, 149
Baru, Sanjaya, 65, 149
Basham, A. L., 29, 149

Basu, Amrita, 87, 126, 149, 153
Baweja, Harinder, 90, 151
Baxter, Craig, 117, 149
Berreman, Gerald D., 97, 130, 149, 150
Beteille, Andre, 44, 49, 51, 150
Bhagavad Gita, 28, 29
Bhakti, 13, 14, 16, 29, 31, 33, 42, 74
Bhargava, Ashok, 60, 150
Bharatiya Janata Party, 37, 38, 69, 86,
  90, 116, 117–118, 125
Bhatty, Zarina, 46, 110, 150
Bose, Sugata, 10, 12, 15, 16, 18, 19, 20,
  21, 23, 126, 150
Bougle, C., 41, 150
Bouton, Marshal M., 131, 150
Bradshaw, York W., 135, 150
Brahma, 13, 28
Brahmanism, 12, 13, 14, 15, 28, 30, 32,
  33, 41, 46, 73, 74, 137
Brahmans, 12, 15, 27, 28, 29, 40, 41, 42,
  48, 95, 96, 124
Brass, Paul R., 117, 121, 123, 150
bride price, 99
bride wealth, 99
British colonial rule, 2, 18, 18–24, 29, 31,
  34, 41, 43, 45. 57, 73, 76, 77, 105, 115
  and caste, 41, 43, 45
  and education, 105
  effect on Indian economy, 57
  effect on Indian religions, 29, 31, 34
  transition from, 115
  transition to, 18–24
  women in, 73, 76, 77
Buddha, 32
Buddhism, 12, 13, 14, 15, 26, 28, 32–33,
  36, 37, 42, 45, 74
  and caste, 42, 45
  emergence and spread of, 12, 13,
    14, 15
  versus Hinduism, 28
  as major Indian religion, 26, 32–33
  and politics, 36, 37
  role of women, 74
Butalia, Urvashi, 150

160

preferential policies, 49–51, 89–91
primary sector, 58
private enterprise, 62, 63, 64, 68, 69, 70
public sector enterprises, 63, 64–65, 69
Punjab, 6, 13, 19, 33, 34, 37, 121–123
purdah, 16, 75
Purusasukta hymn, 27

Q

Qur'an, 31, 86

R

Ragin, Charles, 156
rail system, 2–3, 19, 20
Ramayana, 26, 28, 74
Rao, M. S. A., 42, 152
Ramaswamy, E. A., 60, 69, 156
Rashtriya Swayamsevak Sangh, 37
reform movement, 19th century, 20–21,
    29–30, 31, 46, 84
regional political parties, 116, 118
regional politics, 24, 119–127
religion in India, 10, 26–38, 136
    Buddhism, 32–33
    Christianity, 34–35
    Hinduism, 27–30
    Islam, 30–32
    Jainism, 32–33
    and nationalism, 35–38
    other religions, 34–35
    and politics, 35–38
    Sikhism, 33–34
    Zoroastgrianism, 34–35
religious texts, 19, 45; see also Vedic texts
Revolt of 1857, 20
Rig Veda, 12; see also Vedic texts
Rogers, John D., 58, 60, 156
romantic love, 93, 94, 97, 98, 138
Rose, Kalima, 156
Roy, Ram Mohun, 21
Rubenstein, James M., 156
Rubin, Barnett R., 63, 156
rural areas, 2–3, 9, 22, 44, 52–53, 66–67,
    102, 107

S

sanskritization, 42, 44
Saraswati, 29
Sathyamurthy, T. V., 64, 156
sati, 75
Satnamis, 42–43
Scheduled Castes, 48, 49, 50, 51, 89, 107
Scheduled Tribes, 48, 49, 50, 51, 89, 107
Schmidt, Karl J., 156
Schwartzberg, Joseph E., 2, 156
secondary sector, 58
secularism, 35, 36, 37, 38, 125, 127
Sekhon, Joti, 88, 156
Sen, Amartya, 66, 81, 82, 106, 107, 151
Sen, Ilina, 83, 129, 156
sex determination tests, 83, 84–85
Seymour, Susan, 99, 100, 102, 103, 110,
    155, 156, 157
Shah, Ghanshyam, 129, 157
Shah, Nandita, 82, 84, 86, 87, 152
Sharia, 19, 31, 97; see also Muslim Law
Sharma, Kamud, 130, 157
Sharma, Ursula, 100, 157
Sheth, D. L., 49, 51, 157
Shiva, 11, 13, 28, 29
Shiva, Vandana, 127, 157
Shotton, John R., 107, 108, 109, 157
Shudras, 12, 27, 32, 40, 41, 42, 49
Sikh nationalism, 122–123
Sikhism, 6, 16, 17, 26, 33–34, 36, 37, 42,
    74, 122
Sikhs, 6, 17, 19, 20, 24, 34, 46, 47, 122–123
Singh, Gobind, 33, 34
Singh, Khushwant, 34, 157
Singh, Simrita Gopal, 90, 157
Smelser, Neil J., 157
social change, 5, 24–25, 134–140
social mobility, 39, 40, 41–42, 52–53, 55;
    see also Sanskritization
social movements, 24, 67, 113, 127–131;
    see also caste and politics; grassroots
    movements; language and politics;
    religion and politics; women's
    movements
social stratification, 39–55
    caste; see caste
socialism, 62